INTERNATIONAL
CONFLICT IN AN
AMERICAN CITY

INTERNATIONAL CONFLICT IN AN AMERICAN CITY

Boston's Irish, Italians, and Jews, 1935-1944

John F. Stack, Jr.

Contributions in Political Science, Number 26
GREENWOOD PRESS
WESTPORT, CONNECTICUT • LONDON, ENGLAND

Library of Congress Cataloging in Publication Data

Stack, John F.
    International conflict in an American city.
    (Contributions in political science; no. 26 ISSN 0147-1066)
    Bibliography: p.
    Includes index.
    1. Irish Americans—Massachusetts—Boston—Politics and government. 2. Italian
Americans—Masssachusetts—Boston—Politics and government. 3. Jews in Boston—
Politics and government. 4. Boston—Ethnic relations. I. Title. II. Series.
F73.9.16S7 301.45'1'0974461 78-73798
ISBN 0-313-20887-5.

Library of Congress Catalog Card Number: 78-73798
ISBN: 0-313-20887-5
ISSN: 0147-1066

First published in 1979

Greenwood Press, Inc.
51 Riverside Avenue, Westport, Connecticut 06880

Printed in the United States of America

10 9 8 7 6 5 4 3 2 1

TO MY MOTHER AND FATHER
AND SISTERS

Contents

Foreword

Despite the horror of assimilationists, Americans do not forget the land of their origin even if it be the land of origin several generations removed, or, in the case of American Jews, a land of origin many centuries removed, though now reestablished. The Carter administration has found itself under severe pressure from Greek Americans over the Cyprus case and under less but nonetheless real pressure from Turkish Americans on the other side of the issue. In recent years Arab Americans mobilized support for the Arab cause in the Middle East in still very ineffective imitation of the support for the Israeli cause. Christian Lebanese have protested thus far in vain against the genocide in their native land; and, as in days long past, Irish American money flows again into the hands of revolutionaries in Ireland.

The republic of Czechoslovakia was founded in Pittsburgh, Pennsylvania. Eamon De Valera was born in Brooklyn. The revolution in India was organized in the state of California. Such historical facts are reasonably well known, but rather little attention has been paid to the subtle and complex dynamics of the relationship between Old World and New; of land of origin and land of allegiance; to the politics of the United States and the politics of the old country. With considerable insight and skill, John F. Stack, Jr., has made a major contribution to this crucial aspect of American pluralism. The most fascinating part of his work, at least for this reader, is his description of the "two-way flow" of influence: American reaction to politics abroad and vice versa. Not only does this flow occur, but the nature and the force of the flow changes through time. As Professor Stack indicates at the end of his book, relationships among these three groups (Irish, Italians, and Jews) in Boston are not now what they were during the depression years. One could well add that if Stack had chosen to look at the Boston Irish a generation earlier, he would have found them in a very different posture in relation to domestic and foreign politics—opposing Woodrow Wilson for his betrayal of Ireland, supporting the cause of Irish independence (to the extent that the contribution was decisive in the outcome), and insisting that only when Ireland took its rightful place in the family nations would Irish Americans be respected by their Anglo-Saxon predecessors on these shores.

They were wrong, of course. The Irish, and particularly the Boston Irish, were not respected by the Brahmins any more after Ireland became free than they were before. So be it. The Brahmins are right; the Irish are incorrigible. Despite notable effort, they continue irrevocably to be Irish.

I find it particularly appealing that Professor Stack's implicit analytic models are dynamic but do not require a presumption of assimilation. The nature of the relationships among the ethnic groups he studies can change as both domestic and foreign contacts change, but that doesn't mean, as any citizen of Boston knows, that the Jews, Irish, and Italians would become like one another. Like so many other ethnic researchers of the younger generation, Professor Stack is refreshingly free from any sense of obligation to argue that all those ugly old ethnic things are withering away. Both more realistic and more hopeful about American pluralism, Professor Stack seems committed to the proposition that the social and political structure of America is broad enough and deep enough to absorb ethnic conflict, whether it be over a piece of the urban social turf or over the relative merits of the respective causes of one's land of origin.

As Professor Stack well knows, I am inclined to think he is a bit too harsh on his own Boston Irish ethnic group. For several generations, Harvard University has vigorously worked to create an unfair stereotype of the Boston Irish among the national intellectual elites, a stereotype that is so pervasive that sometimes I think the Boston Irish half believe it themselves and feel constrained to live up to it. (In a somewhat different context, Richard Stivers has argued that Irish drinking behavior in part is an attempt to live up to a stereotype.) Heaven forfend that a Chicago Irishman like me should attempt to defend the Boston Irish, particularly against the mild criticisms of one of their own, but I must note that the myth of the McCarthyite (Joe, not Eugene) Irish bigot, so dear to the heart of the nation's intellectual and cultural elites, is simply not sustained in national sample data and I suspect would not be sustained by survey data in Boston either. Mind you, the Boston Irish are not saints (I am sure Professor Stack would agree), but—faint compliment from a Chicagoan—they are no worse than the Italians or Jews of Boston.

This minor point of chauvinism aside, Professor Stack's book will make fascinating reading for all of those of us who have been hooked on the study of ethnicity. And for a few of us who are of a somewhat earlier generation than Professor Stack, it will bring back memories of roast beef, mashed potatoes, and gravy on a Sunday afternoon and the rich voice of Charles Coughlin on the radio, a voice that my New Deal Democrat Irish Catholic father, with my enthusiastic support, turned off for the much better entertainment of the then fabulous Chicago Bears.

Andrew M. Greeley

Acknowledgments

Without the support and encouragement of Andrew M. Greeley and Fred A. Sondermann this study could not have been completed. Andrew Greeley provided me with challenging and thoughtful criticisms through several drafts of the manuscript. Fred Sondermann introduced me to the study of international politics and has offered probing questions and careful evaluations of the linkages between ethnicity and international politics. James P. Piscatori read the entire manuscript and provided me with stimulating and insightful comments. Arthur N. Gilbert and Robert C. Good contributed a number of important ideas. Cynthia H. Enloe read the first chapter and provided me with valuable comments. Joyce R. Lilie offered me important advice on style.

A number of scholars patiently answered my questions and generously gave of their time: Daniel Bell, Paul R. Brass, Thomas N. Brown, Richard B. Finnegan, Lawrence Fuchs, Oscar Handlin, James J. Kenneally, Anthony P. Maingot, Michael Novak, and Anthony Richmond.

I want to thank a number of individuals and institutions. Y. T. Feng and Francis Maloney and their staff at the Boston Public Library were most helpful to me in my quest for data. Alan Fox of the Massachusetts State Library provided me with a number of excellent sources and insights into Boston of the 1930s and 1940s.

Bishop Dailey, chancellor of the Archdiocese of Boston, made the papers of William Henry O'Connell available to me. James J. Kenneally of Stonehill College directed me to a number of valuable files in the papers of Congressman Joseph Martin. I am grateful for the help and assistance of Jerome Bakst and his staff at the Anti-Defamation League of B'nai B'rith, New York, New York, for granting me permission to use a number of newspaper files on anti-Semitism in Boston. In addition, I want to express my gratitude to Bernard Wax, director of the American Jewish Historical Society, and Robert Lovett of the Baker Library, Harvard University. I am grateful to Mina K. Curtiss for granting me permission to quote from the papers of her father, Louis Kirstein. My thanks to the staffs of the Boston College Archives; the Cushing-Martin Library, Stonehill College; the Dinand Library, Holy Cross College; the Harvard University Archives; Muggar Library, Boston University; and the New York Public Library.

I am grateful for the encouragement of a number of friends and colleagues: Lucille Seibert Brennan, Mary Volcansek, Judson M. DeCew, Jr., Thomasine Kushner, Anthony P. Maingot, John P. Paul, Jesus M. Pedre-Crespo, and Mark D. Szuchman. I am indebted to James P. Piscatori and Mark B. Rosenberg who provided me with constant support during the writing of this study.

The Graduate School of International Studies of the University of Denver and its Center for the Study of International Race Relations were generous in their financial support of the research for this study.

Finally, Howard and Lisa Mandel provided editorial assistance. Barbara Murray and Diana Richardson typed earlier drafts of the manuscript. Gertrude MacDonald Masterson typed the final manuscript with patience and care.

INTERNATIONAL CONFLICT IN AN AMERICAN CITY

1

Introduction

This is a study of the Irish, Italians, and Jews of Boston as they reacted to a number of issues of the 1930s and 1940s—fascism, Nazism, anti-Semitism, isolationism, and the coming of World War II. Its basic argument is that the international system served as a catalyst for the outbreak of ethnic conflict among Boston's Irish, Italians, and Jews. This study takes issue with the traditional notion that world politics is exclusively comprised of over one hundred and fifty sovereign, indivisible, and independent entities called states. Rather, it argues that world politics in the twentieth century is a patchwork of actors that include states as well as nongovernmental organizations such as multinational corporations and ethnic groups. Because ethnicity transcends the boundaries of states, ethnic groups may become directly involved in world politics.

Ethnicity is an amazingly complex and difficult phenomenon to analyze. Part of the problem in grappling with the concept is that it has become so broad as to be analytically useless.[1] A further difficulty is that anything in the way of a general theory of interethnic relations has not yet evolved.[2] What the student of ethnicity confronts is bits and pieces of concepts strewn about the conceptual and descriptive landscape. The purpose of this introductory chapter is to raise a number of issues—the organization of the

ethnic group, the interplay between ethnicity and politics, and the
transnational dimensions of ethnicity—pertaining to the dynamics
of ethnicity generally and to ethnicity in Boston specifically.
Definitions of ethnicity abound in the literature of the social
sciences. Richard A. Schermerhorn proposes a broadly representative one. For Schermerhorn *ethnicity* refers to

> . . .a collectivity within a larger society having real or putative com-
> mon ancestry, memories of a shared historical past, and a cultural
> focus on one or more symbolic elements defined as the epitome of
> their peoplehood. Examples of such symbolic elements are: kinship
> patterns, physical contiguity (as in localism or sectionalism), reli-
> gious affiliation, languages or dialect forms, tribal affiliations, na-
> tionality, phenotypical features, or any combination of these. A
> necessary accompaniment is some consciousness of kind among
> members of the group.[3]

Schermerhorn emphasizes two important aspects of ethnicity. The
first is its primordial quality—the expression of a sense of peoplehood. The second refers to the structural dynamics of the ethnic
group and the broader political, social, and economic environment
in which it interacts. Students of ethnicity are now beginning to
probe the nature of the relationships between the primordial and
the structural dynamics of ethnic identity.[4] It is evident that the primordial attributes of ethnicity regularly interact with the structural
dimensions of the larger society. Indeed, the interplay between primordial and structural variables helps to define ethnicity. How ex-
actly this interplay occurs is crucial to an understanding of ethnicity in Boston during the 1930s and 1940s because the reactions of
Boston's Irish, Italians, and Jews to the international system were
influenced by each group's "life history."

PRIMORDIAL DYNAMICS

For primordialists, a sense of peoplehood forms the basis of the
ethnic experience. Ethnicity becomes an expression of a "basic
group identity."[5] It is basic in that fundamental human attributes
are transmitted from one generation to the next. It is a group identi-

ty because it binds the individual to larger collectivities. As Clifford Geertz points out: "But for virtually every person, in every society, at almost all times, some attachments seem to flow more from a sense of the natural—some would say spiritual—affinity than from social interaction."[6] For Geertz and other primordialists, these "natural affinities" become the immutable dimensions of ethnicity whether they are characterized by cultural, linguistic, religious, regional, or customary identifications. By embracing the realm of deeply felt sentiments and emotions, primordial stirrings are made concrete and placed in a historical framework. This, in part, accounts for the extraordinary power and potency of ethnic ties.

But ethnicity is more than dimly perceived emotions recalling a primordial past. Ethnicity becomes a powerful identity merging the individual with the group. In its most constructive moments, ethnicity provides an answer to the question, "Who am I?" The ethnic group can reassure the individual that "in the deepest and most literal sense...he is not *alone*, which is what all but a very few human beings most fear to be."[7] In sheltering the individual from loneliness, the ethnic group may provide him with a sense of self-esteem—to reassure him that his life has meaning and worth.

The irony is that even as ethnicity contributes to an individual's self-worth by placing a strong positive value on the "we," it may have profoundly destructive effects by emphasizing the "they." As the bloody history of ethnic conflicts in the twentieth century illustrates, a consciousness of kind is often accompanied by a recognition of the differences that divide mankind. The critical danger is that once primordial aspirations are aroused, they will not easily abate. Thus ethnicity is a double-edged sword. It may contribute to the enhancement of the group or it may just as easily result in the further brutalization of humanity.

Undoubtedly, the structure of a specific ethnic group and society will provide some insights into the enlightening and dehumanizing effects of ethnicity. For the primordialists, however, the most important dimension of ethnicity becomes the enduring nature of a sense of peoplehood. It is, as Geertz argues, one of the "givens—of social existence," an undeniable aspect of humanity.[8] In accepting the universality of ethnic aspirations, the primordialists fail to explain why ethnicity disappears during one historical period and re-

appears in another. In emphasizing the immutable human characteristics of ethnicity, there is a danger that one becomes an advocate rather than an analyst.[9] Although it seems clear that primordial ties exist and form a critical component of ethnicity, they fail
to explain a number of crucial dynamics of ethnicity. To try to con-
ceptualize ethnicity more fully, we need to look to the structure of
the ethnic group as well as the dynamics of the society in which it
interacts. Boston's Irish and Vietnam's Montagnards may both constitute ethnic groups, but their political capacities and behavior will
differ in part because of the differences in their respective internal
organizations, stratifications, culture, and so on. There are a
number of significant structural variables.

INTERNAL STRUCTURE

First, the institutional completeness of the group is a key dimension of ethnicity.[10] *Institutional completeness* refers to the internal
organization of the ethnic group—how the group is structured, the
institutions that contribute to the maintenance of a distinctive culture, and the degree to which the ethnic group intermeshes with the
prevailing structures of the larger environment. The institutional
completeness of an ethnic group may range from informal networks of personal contacts to a formally structured society within a
society. In its most extreme form an institutionally complete ethnic
group would satisfy all the physical and psychological needs of its
members. In most cases, the crucial dimension is not the extent of
institutional completeness but that the ethnic group has some institutions that give tangible expression to a sense of group identity
rather than none at all.[11] But any ethnic group, such as the Boston
Irish or Boston Black communities, are not fixed institutionally.
They are historical phenomena, which means the institutional completeness of Irish and Blacks in Boston can increase or decrease over
time.

Religious organizations, an ethnic press (particularly if the ethnic
group has a different language), fraternal clubs, and social welfare
organizations help to form the main institutional structures of the
ethnic group and thus contribute to the maintenance of group solidarity. The extent of institutional completeness becomes particularly

important when immigration has declined and the population of the group has stabilized. Thus the principal organizations of the ethnic group provide a focal point for the life of the group by raising "new issues or [activating] old ones for public debate."[12] Moreover, the institutions of the group tangibly express group boundaries while reinforcing a sense of peoplehood through readily identifiable symbols.

In most cases, the institutional completeness of an ethnic group tends to increase the cohesion of the group. The building of group solidarity, however, need not take place at the expense of full or partial integration into the institutions of the dominant group. Ethnic boundaries are surprisingly fluid and resilient. The precise outcome of group cohesion rests on a number of specific conditions. For example, the institutional completeness of Boston's Irish community tended to retard Irish integration into the city's Yankee and Jewish communities. When the Irish arrived in Boston throughout the middle and late nineteenth century, the city's Yankee-dominated political, economic, and social institutions were closed to them. Between 1850 and 1900 the Irish worked to establish as complete a society within a society as possible. The Boston Irish were so successful that they erected a society with institutions paralleling almost every aspect of the dominant society.[13]

By the turn of the century, the institutional completeness of Irish Boston, which was initially created as a means of physical and psychological survival, had been rigidly institutionalized. It acted as a barrier to the integration of the Irish into the life of non-Irish Boston. Although the Irish captured the city's bureaucratic and political organizations, integration into Boston's socioeconomic and cultural institutions remained closed to them. Irish isolation, in part, resulted from Yankee discrimination both active and structural but the institutional structure of the Irish community also reduced contacts between Irish and Yankees. The Boston Irish generously supported a sprawling religious organization of churches, social welfare organizations, and an incredibly costly school system. This probably drained enormous sums of money that might have generated upward socioeconomic mobility. Cultural norms, in part, defined by the institutional structure of Boston's Irish community, emphasized values and skills, for example, involvement in politics, law, and insurance rather than corporate finance, that reduced

nonprofessional contacts with the host society.[14] Moreover, Irish
religious and political elites throughout the first three decades of
the twentieth century employed divisive strategies that tended to
alienate the Boston Irish from every other group in the city.

A contrasting case is that of Boston's Jewish community. The institutional completeness of Jewish Boston positively aided Jewish
integration into Boston's Yankee-dominated cultural, social, and
financial institutions. Whereas the institutional completeness of
Boston's Jewish community ultimately fostered the cohesion of the
group through its religious life, fraternal orders, social welfare
organizations, and newspapers (particularly in the face of the intensifying Nazi Holocaust), the institutional structure promoted the
integration of Jews into the institutions of Boston's Yankee community. Through patterns of upward socioeconomic mobility, remarkable educational achievements, and liberal social welfare
values, Boston's Jews gained entrance into many of the inner sanc-
tums of Yankee Boston. Thus the solidarity of an ethnic group need
not exclude expanded contacts with other collectivities on both personal and group levels. As the work of anthropologist Fredrik
Barth illustrated, ethnic boundaries are often permeable, permitting social interaction across group lines without the weakening
or disappearance of the ethnic group.[15]

The principal institutions of an ethnic group do not exist in a
vacuum, of course. Socioeconomic stratifications within and
among ethnic groups (class), different levels of social and occupational prestige (status), and cultural diversity have immediate bearing on the institutional completeness of an ethnic group. For example, class, status, and cultural differences bred antagonisms between middle-class German Jewish residents of New York City and
the arriving hordes of poor East European Jews in the late nineteenth and early twentieth centuries. The tensions between German
and East European Jews lingered for more than two generations in
New York notwithstanding an extensive and growing panoply of
Jewish organizations. Without doubt, the institutional completeness of a group is a key dimension of ethnicity. So, too, are the
group's cultural values, the structural dynamics of the larger society, and the political system in which ethnic groups interact.

Cultural values form the second dimension of ethnicity. *Culture* is defined as a common set of beliefs, values, norms, ideas, and symbols that help to differentiate right from wrong. "Cultural bonds grow out of men's recognition of their own standards of behavior and prizing of those standards to the extent that they feel most comfortable and secure when among persons sharing them."[16] Culture reinforces a sense of peoplehood but it transcends the realm of primordial instincts by giving tangible expression to group differences in manners, accents, attitudes, and ideas. Consequently, culture serves a critical role in keeping alive the communal life of the ethnic group. It may provide individuals with a psychological anchor by reaffirming an individual and collective sense of destiny in times of turmoil. Similarly, cultural bonds may help to maintain the boundaries of the ethnic group by providing its members with tangible reminders of their distinctive identity. Culture, therefore, ranges in various degrees of intensity. Whereas a network of regular communication and interaction is generally necessary for a group to have a strong communal life, cultural values may persist on a subconscious level over a number of generations. An example of the subconscious persistence of cultural traits would be the case of Irish Americans. As a group, Irish Americans share little in the way of a distinctive communal culture in the 1970s. But ongoing political and sociological research suggest that Irish cultural traits continue to persist in a number of areas: in patterns of alcohol consumption, career choices, and in an informal and personalized approach to politics.[17]

The resilience and fluidity of cultural boundaries do not exist in a vacuum. Culture must be examined alongside the institutional completeness of the ethnic group and the overall social structure of the dominant society. Indeed, it appears likely that distinctive values contribute to the evolution of the formal institutions of the ethnic group whereas the institutional completeness of the group reinforces the distinctiveness of its communal identity. Thus culture is a vital component of ethnicity and must be examined in light of the organization of the ethnic group as well as the structure of the host society.

The interaction between the ethnic group and the social structure of the dominant society is the third dimension of ethnicity. *Social structure* refers to the dominant values, beliefs, and norms of a society. They are manifest in the educational systems, the mass media, and patterns of socioeconomic mobility. The resources of the ethnic group, its stratification within the society (its dominance or subordinance relative to other groups), and the prevailing levels of conflict within the society are relevant variables as well. The type of political system is a key structure and is treated separately below. In each case, the relationships between an ethnic group and the social structure of the dominant society involve a number of different factors. "In particular societies, and in different regions, there are different polarizing issues, rooted in the dominance structures of these societies, and only the historical nature of these structures and the issues at hand define the specific divisions and confrontations in those societies."[18] This study is in part an attempt to analyze those factors contributing to the outbreak of ethnic conflict in Boston. In America, however, there are three explicit models of the interplay between the ethnic group and the host society that have dominated the study of ethnicity for a number of years. Each model diminishes the importance of ethnicity.

MODELS OF ETHNIC INTERACTION

The most widely known model is that of the *melting pot*. It suggests that an "American culture" is a synthesis of the contributions of each immigrant group over time. It presumes that American culture is malleable and that the end product of the process is a "new American," a composite of the strengths of each group.[19] In reality, however, the idea of the melting pot has meant only a superficial sharing of cultural traits among different groups. Far from being an amalgamation of different traits, the melting-pot ideal suggests the dominance of a white, Anglo-Saxon, Protestant (WASP) culture. The melting pot is not premised on the sharing of traits but the realization of irreversible trends toward assimilation. To become American, one must forsake the traditional ways of the ethnic group and embrace the dominant values of American society. The social structure of WASP America becomes the critical variable. Immigrants and their children become American whether or not they like it—the power of the mass media, the educational system, and the job market cannot be resisted for long.

The second model sees the explicit *domination and oppression* of ethnic and racial groups as the key structural dimension of America.[20] The dominant society acts in a coercive fashion to eradicate a group's indigenous culture. In this perspective, WASP America pursues strategies similar to the European colonization of Africa and Asia in the nineteenth and twentieth centuries. The historical experiences of the American Indians, Blacks, and Orientals are cited as evidence of this model.

The third model views *class affiliations* as the main structural dynamic of American society. Ethnicity is viewed as a weak, transitory, and ultimately irrational basis of group mobilization. Class ties, in contrast, represent a legitimate historically defined basis of group organization in the nineteenth and twentieth centuries.

In each of the three models, the disappearance of ethnicity is assumed to be a given. Each model thus prejudges the outcome of a process that is by no means complete as the reintensification of ethnic allegiances in the 1960s and 1970s illustrate. Moreover, the three models of interethnic relations infuse the study of ethnicity with research agendas that discourage inquiry into the nature and persistence of ethnicity. Once ethnicity becomes the dependent variable in any analysis of the social structure of the United States, assimilation becomes a foregone conclusion.[21] This is not to dismiss the homogenizing aspects of modern American culture, which are apparent everywhere. However, it is to assert that just as third-generation Irishmen or Poles may be more alike than their grandparents in their understanding of American cultural values (as disseminated through the mass media), they may be, simultaneously, more different from their ancestors. Whereas the grandparents were probably peasants, the grandchildren may have totally different occupational and educational preferences.[22] Indeed, the differences in attitudes and values may be more stiking than those of their ancestors. If the homogenizing currents of American social structure were as powerful as the melting pot, domination-oppression, and class models suggest, the differences between third-generation ethnics should not be salient. But as Andrew M. Greeley argues, "Certain differences rooted in historical heritages may persist between the two Americans with no sign of diminution."[23] The persistence of such ethnic differences suggests, therefore, that the processes of ethnic differentiation and assimilation proceed simultaneously.

This proposition views the social structure of the United States as being remarkably tolerant of group diversity.

The societalwide acceptance of group pluralism probably reflects the federal structure of the American political system, which encouraged the participation of groups through a process of compromise and coalition building.[24] Although ethnic groups have been the objects of intense nativism at various times in American history, the formal governmental structures of the United States, at least, did not discourage the formation of ethnic collectivities to pursue political ends. Indeed, the political system seemed to suggest that it was in the best interests of ethnic groups to organize along these lines.[25] Thus the ethnic group played a critical role in helping immigrants and their children to adjust to life in America. It functioned as a kind of psychological halfway house easing the initial shocks and strains of the immigration process, reaffirming the worth of traditional ethnic values and beliefs, and adapting to many broad cultural tenets of life in the United States.

The ethnic group was, in other words, a highly functional social unit. It provided members with a natural arena in which political and economic skills could be developed.[26] It played a role in socioeconomic mobility by offering immigrants information on jobs and often providing its members with a place to develop important skills.[27] During times when the institutions of the host society were closed to immigrants and their children, the ethnic group provided a place where its members could live, work, and achieve recognition. But even as the ethnic group assisted in the adjustment and acculturation of immigrants in the United States, the group did not form an impenetrable barrier to integration with the institutions of the dominant society.[28] Ethnicity functioned as a permeable individual and collective identity, sometimes salient and at other times less than significant. Undoubtedly, the social structure of the United States permitted and encouraged the flexibility of ethnic identities. In this environment, ethnicity became an effective basis of group mobilization simply because it could adjust to the needs of its members as well as to the more inclusive social structures of American life. Rigidly defined ethnic enclaves did not evolve in the United States for the descendants of white European immigrants as they did in the urban Black ghettos or Indian reservations. This process has nowhere been better viewed than in the political process. The interplay between the political system and the ethnic group is our final variable.

ETHNICITY AND POLITICS

The political process is a key variable for three reasons. First, the political system ultimately oversees the allocation of resources among competing ethnic groups in any society. "Status competition is diffuse and lacks a specific site. Economic competition is dispersed between interests and occupations. . . ."[29] Thus the political system becomes the central arena in which ethnic conflicts and rivalries are manifest. Hence the political process is one of the most important avenues for the mobilization of ethnic-group interests.

Second, there has been a steady accretion of power in the political systems of most advanced industrial societies during the last fifty years. Economic, cultural, and social systems have become subordinate to politics. This is particularly evident in the economic sector where economic issues are ultimately governed by political needs.[30] The political process becomes the final arbiter among conflicting values subsumed under the heading "quality of life"—social welfare, environmental, economic, ethnic.[31]

Third, in the developing world the political process is the focal point of virtually all activities within a state. The process of modernization requires the restructuring of a society from the top down.[32] Hence decisions made by central elites are political in nature almost by definition. Here questions involving the distribution of scarce resources in multiethnic societies frame ethnic cleavages throughout the developing world. Thus ethnicity combines two attributes that interact with politics throughout the world.

The first is the intensity of affective ties (a sense of peoplehood or belonging).[33] The institutional completeness of the ethnic group, the social structure of the host society, the nature of the ethnic group's culture, all have a bearing on the intensity of ethnicity. Once ethnicity is manifest, however, the political process provides an arena in which passions can be aroused and intensified as ethnic conflict throughout the developing world illustrates—in the affluent oil-exporting states, the middle-income countries typified by Brazil, or the bulk of the desperately poor nations of Africa and Asia. The salience of ethnicity throughout the world is an inescapable aspect of politics. In this context, a sense of peoplehood—the intensity of affective ties—is a variable that must be reckoned with by participants in the political process. In the 1930s, for example, there was a marked increase in ethnic solidarity and conflict in a number of American cities. In Boston, New York, and Detroit, the Irish, Italians, and Jews sought comfort from the psychological and physical hardships of the Great Depression.[34] In an era when resources were severely limited—social welfare benefits, jobs, housing, and food—ethnic conflicts increased. Ethnic groups thought in terms of the "we" as threatened by outsiders. But the reintensification of affective ties is not limited to disadvantaged groups in times of socioeconomic upheaval. In the advanced societies of the West, amid unprecedented affluence, the salience of ethnicity has dramatically increased. The steadily increasing bureaucratization of business, industry, and labor in postindustrial societies has been accompanied by the isolation and alienation of individuals and groups throughout the West.[35] Ethnic reawakenings have attempted to provide individuals with a sense of community conspicuously absent from their daily lives.

Second, ethnicity constitutes an effective means of group mobilization.[36] Since the political arena has come to dominate the life of most societies throughout the world, the cohesiveness of the ethnic group becomes a natural community of interests. Ethnic groups put forward demands for the allocation of resources and values that are frequently successful.

Consequently, ethnic groups combine both affective ties and instrumental goals that increase the viability of the group throughout the world. This is not to suggest, however, the ethnicity is the only basis of group mobilization. Historically, socioeconomic (class) interests have fulfilled that function. Nor is it to suggest that ethnicity is unaffected by other identities, such as class ties, within a society. "Socio-economic classes and ethnic groups are analytically separate, though in practice they continually intertwine."[37] Sometimes class cleavages are congruent with ethnicity. "More often than not, in the advanced countries at least, ethnicity cuts across class lines and members of different ethnic groups are both in the economic majority and economic minority."[38] It may be that as class cleavages decline in salience, ethnic ties become more intense.[39] The presence of cross-cutting socioeconomic cleavages tempers the tendency to view ethnicity—both its affective and instrumental dimensions—as an immutable factor in the political and sociological organization of group life.

Historical conditions, the social structure of the dominant society, and the precise nature of the ethnic group are variables that help to define ethnic identity. But ethnicity is not confined to the internal structure of a particular state. The global system may play a surprisingly important role. This study attempts to define that role for the case of Boston.

ETHNICITY AND WORLD POLITICS

Traditionally, American social scientists have relegated the ethnic dimensions of world politics to the investigation of foreign policy issues—Irish antipathy for Great Britain, Jewish support for the state of Israel, and East European demands for the liberation of their "captive" homelands. On the whole, these studies viewed the machinations of American ethnic groups as examples of interest-group politics.[40] Little systematic attention was paid to the possible relationships between world politics and the genesis of ethnicity aside from foreign policy concerns. Moreover, there was often an explicit assumption that foreign-policy issues would decline in salience as ethnic groups were assimilated into the mainstream of American culture. It was argued that the assimilation of America's diverse immigrant populations, over the course of several generations, would solve the problems that ethnic groups posed to the making of American foreign policy.[41] However, the expected assimilation of the descendants of European immigrants did not occur while ethnic groups continued to participate in the making of foreign policy.

The assimilationist perspective employed by many students of American foreign policy not only misjudged the nature of ethnicity in the United States but oversimplified the dynamics of world politics by viewing states as the only significant actors in the global system. This conceptualization of world politics is best illustrated in the *state-centric model*, which suggests that the global system resembles a billiards table. States are analogous to billiard balls colliding with one another, forming and reforming different configurations within the system. Foreign policy processes, therefore, become the only available avenues through which domestic groups could influence the global system. The state-centric model does not reflect global realities in a century characterized by ever-increasing patterns of interdependence and political, economic, cultural, and psychological penetration of states.

In this fluid environment, subnational groups may interact directly with states and other actors. The concept of *transnationalism*— the movement of tangible or intangible items across state lines when at least one actor is not a state or intergovernmental organization—offers an alternative approach for the study of world politics.[42] The notion of transnationalism does not reject the influence exerted by states but suggests a more complex and subtle framework for the analysis of world politics. From this perspective a number of variables ranging from ideas and attitudes to the proliferation of global technology play a significant role in world politics.[43] Thus subnational actors, ethnic groups for example, may interact with states and other global actors—international organizations, multinational corporations, the Catholic church, or the Ford Foundation. Indeed, the doctrine of national self-determination, the demands of ethnic separatists, and the existence of global communication and transportation networks throughout the twentieth century document the steadily increasing visibility of ethnic groups as transnational actors in world politics.

This book analyzes the interplay of domestic and international factors that resulted in ethnic conflict in Boston between 1935 and 1944.[44] It examines the dynamics of ethnicity among Boston's Irish, Italians, and Jews through an evaluation of the institutional completeness and culture of each group as well as the social structure and political systems in which they interacted. The second dimension of this study evaluates the ways in which the international system directly intervened in Boston during the 1930s and 1940s.

NOTES

1. Orlando Patterson, "Context and Choice in Ethnic Allegiance: A Theoretical Framework and Caribbean Case Study," in *Ethnicity, Theory and Experience*, ed. Nathan Glazer and Daniel P. Moynihan (Cambridge: Harvard University Press, 1975), pp. 305-13.

2. Michael Hechter, "Theories of Interethnic Relations," in "Ethnicity in a Changing World," ed. John F. Stack, Jr. (Unpublished manuscript).

3. R.A. Schermerhorn, *Comparative Ethnic Relations, A Framework for Theory and Research* (New York: Random House, 1970), p. 123.

4. See, for example, the collection of papers contained in the anthology edited by Leo A. Despres, *Ethnicity and Resource Competition in Plural Societies* (The Hague: Mouton Publishers, 1975), particularly Despres's concluding essay, "Toward a Theory of Ethnic Phenomena," pp. 187-207.

5. Harold Isaacs, *The Idols of the Tribe, Group Identity and Political Change* (New York: Harper & Row, 1975).

6. Clifford Geertz, "The Integrative Revolution, Primordial Sentiments and Civil Politics in the New States," in *The Interpretation of Cultures*, ed. Clifford Geertz (New York: Basic Books, 1973), pp. 259-60.

7. Isaacs, *Idols of the Tribe*, p. 43.

8. Geertz, "The Integrative Revolution," p. 258.

9. Nathan Glazer and Daniel P. Moynihan, Introduction to *Ethnicity, Theory and Experience*, ed. Glazer and Moynihan, p. 20.

10. Raymond Breton, "Institutional Completeness of Ethnic Communities and the Personal Relations of Immigrants," *American Journal of Sociology* 70, no. 2 (September 1964):193-205.

11. Ibid., p. 201.

12. Ibid., p. 199.

13. See Oscar Handlin's classic study, *Boston's Immigrants, A Study in Acculturation*, rev. and enl. ed. (New York: Atheneum, 1970).

14. Andrew M. Greeley's work points to the persistence of ethnic traits among America's diverse Irish American communities. See *That Most Distressful Nation, The Taming of American Irish* (Chicago: Quadrangle Books, 1972), *Ethnicity in the United States: A Preliminary Reconnaissance* (New York: John Wiley & Sons, 1974), and *The American Catholic, A Social Portrait* (New York: Basic Books, 1977).

15. Fredrik Barth, Introduction to *Ethnic Groups and Boundaries*, ed. Fredrik Barth (Boston: Little, Brown & Co., 1969), pp. 9-38.

16. Cynthia Enloe, *Ethnic Conflict and Political Development* (Boston: Little, Brown & Co., 1973), p. 15.

17. Greeley, *The American Catholic*, pp. 253-69. See also James Q. Wilson and Edward C. Banfield, "Political Ethos Revisited," *American Political Science Review* 65 (December 1971):1048-62; and Terry Nicholas Clark, "The Irish Ethnic and the Spirit of Patronage," *Ethnicity* 4 (December 1975):305-59.

18. Daniel Bell, "Ethnicity and Social Change," in *Ethnicity, Theory and Experience*, ed. Glazer and Moynihan, p. 159.

19. For an incisive review of the literature, see Andrew M. Greeley, "Models for Viewing American Catholicism," in Greeley, *The American Catholic*, pp. 9-21.

20. Robert Blauner, "Internal Colonialism and Ghetto Revolt," *Social Problems* 16 (Spring 1968):395-408. See also Nathan Glazer, "Blacks and Ethnic Groups: The Difference and the Political Difference It Makes," *Social Problems* 18, no. 4 (Spring 1971):444-61.

21. Greeley, *The American Catholic*, p. 15.

22. Ibid.

23. Ibid.

24. Michael Kammen, *People of Paradox* (New York: Random House; Vintage Press, 1972); Greeley, *The American Catholic*, p. 19.

25. Ibid.

26. Ibid.

27. Michael Hechter, "Toward a Theory of Ethnic Change," *Politics and Society* 2, no. 1 (Fall 1971):42-43.

28. Greeley's ethnogenesis model is the most complete conceptualization of the persistence of ethnicity in American society to date. See *The American Catholic*, pp. 22-30.

29. Bell, "Ethnicity and Social Change," p. 161.

30. Ibid., pp. 161-62.

31. Ibid.

32. Ibid.

33. Ibid., p. 169.

34. See, for example, Charles H. Trout, "Boston During the Great Depression 1928-1940" (Ph.D. diss., Columbia University, 1972); Ronald H. Bayor, *Neighbors in Conflict, The Irish, Germans, Jews, and Italians of New York City, 1929-1941* (Baltimore: Johns Hopkins University Press, 1978); John P. Diggins, *Mussolini and Fascism, The View from America* (Princeton: Princeton University Press, 1973); and John F. Stack, Jr., "The City as a Symbol of International Conflict: Boston's Irish, Italians and Jews, 1935-1944" (Ph.D. diss., University of Denver, 1977).

35. Bell, "Ethnicity and Social Change," pp. 161-69.

36. Ibid., p. 169.

37. Enloe, *Ethnic Conflict and Political Development*, p. 27.

38. Bell, "Ethnicity and Social Change," p. 168.

39. Ibid.

40. Louis L. Gerson's *The Hyphenate in Recent American Politics and Diplomacy* (Lawrence: University of Kansas Press, 1964), is perhaps the most representative study.

41. Thomas A. Bailey, *The Man in the Street: The Impact of American Public Opinion on Foreign Policy* (New York: Macmillan Co., 1948).

42. Joseph S. Nye, Jr., and Robert O. Keohane, "Transnational Relations and World Politics: An Introduction," in *Transnational Relations and World Politics*, ed. Robert O. Keohane and Joseph S. Nye, Jr. (Cambridge: Harvard University Press, 1972), p. xii.

43. For a more detailed discussion of ethnicity and transnationalism, see John F. Stack, Jr., "Ethnic Groups as Emerging Transnational Actors," in *Ethnic Identities in a Transnational World*, ed. John F. Stack, Jr. (Westport, Conn: Greenwood Press, forthcoming).

44. For a cogent analysis of the dynamics of ethnic conflict, see Bayor, *Neighbors in Conflict*, fn. 2, p. 168.

2

The Setting of the City:
Boston's Irish, Italians, and Jews

The massive influx of impoverished Irish, Italian, and Jewish immigrants throughout the nineteenth century left an indelible imprint on Boston's political, socioeconomic, and cultural development. This chapter considers four historical dimensions of ethnicity in Boston to provide a framework for the analysis of ethnic conflict in the 1930s and 1940s. They are: (1) the Brahmin reaction to immigration; (2) socioeconomic characteristics of Boston's ethnic communities; (3) Boston's political system; and (4) interethnic cultural relations.

BRAHMINS AND IMMIGRANTS

To analyze ethnicity in Boston, consider the impact of immigration on the city's influential cultural, socioeconomic, and ethnic elite—the Brahmins. Historically, the old stock residents of Boston, many with colonial origins, dominated the city's life. Gradually, Boston's native-born citizens evolved into two distinct communities. The majority of Anglo-American descendants, the Yankees, formed a community of skilled artisans, tradesmen, shopkeepers, and civil servants.[1] In contrast, the Brahmins constituted a small, self-conscious elite based on inherited wealth in trade, fishing, finance, and manufacturing. They cultivated a distinctive sense of history and *noblesse oblige* that contributed to the flowering of a remarkable "New England" culture in the seventeenth, eighteenth, and nineteenth centuries. In literature, the arts, education, and social service, Brahmin contributions earned for Boston the well-deserved reputation as a major cultural and intellectual center of American life. The flattering title of the "Athens of America" aptly conveyed the image that the city's Brahmin culture projected to the nation and the world. Although Brahmins and Yankees differed from each other in socioeconomic status, a strong sense of kinship based on common ancestry and shared historical experiences transcended cultural differences that were expressed in wealth, accents, and manners.[2] As the heirs of impressive New England cultural traditions, the Brahmins assumed the political and social leadership of Boston's Yankee community. But it was the arrival of hordes of Irish immigrants fleeing the misery of the Irish famine in the latter years of the 1840s and 1850s that eventually strengthened the ethnic ties that bound Yankees and Brahmins together.

The influx of impoverished Irish immigrants traumatized the city. The number of Irish residents of Boston grew rapidly from 3,936 in 1840 to 28,917 in 1849. Between 1849 and 1850 over 15,000 Irish immigrants poured into the city. By 1855 there were more than 50,000 Irish immigrants living in unspeakable poverty in Boston's waterfront slums.[3] The immobility and squalid living conditions of the Boston Irish transformed that beautiful and aristocratic city "recasting its boundaries and disfiguring its physical appearance; by their poverty they introduced problems of disease, vice, and crime, with which neither they nor the community were ready to cope."[4] The Irish assault on Boston did not provoke Brahmin xenophobia and nativism until after 1860, however. The egalitarian traditions of the Adamses and of Hancock and Emerson persisted in spite of the unpleasant burdens that Irish immigration presented to the Brahmins. These proper Bostonians deplored the excesses of anti-Catholic and anti-Irish hysteria during the 1840s and 1850s.[5]

It was only "until the ideals of the newcomers threatened to replace those of the old society," as Oscar Handlin observed, that the Brahmins rejected their long-established traditions of political tolerance. "At that moment the tradition of tolerance was breached and long repressed hostilities found highly inflammable expression."[6] The political ascendancy of Boston's large and sprawling Irish population constituted the principal catalyst resulting in Brahmin xenophobia. The trials of Charles Francis Adams, Jr., scion of two presidents of the United States and a host of other Boston luminaries, illustrated the Brahmin perspective. In 1893 Adams reluctantly moved from the beloved ancestral home in Quincy, Massachusetts, to rural Lincoln, Massachusetts, to escape Irish political dominance in the town of his ancestors. Adams bitterly resented the Irish and Italian immigrants who had displaced him from the birthplace of his ancestors.[7] Like other Brahmins of his generation he looked with growing suspicion and dread on the increasing immigrant populations in the United States.

The long-term effects of Irish immigration deeply affected the Brahmin culture, as Handlin noted:

> The economic, physical, and intellectual development of the town accentuated the division between the Irish and the rest of the population and engendered fear of foreign groups whose appalling slums had already destroyed the beauty of a fine city and whose appalling ideas threatened the fondest conceptions of universal progress, of grand reform, and a regenerated mankind. The vague discomforts and the latent distrusts produced by the problems of these strangers festered in the unconscious mind of the community for many years. Though its overt manifestations were comparatively rare, the social uneasiness was none the less real.[8]

The most intense Irish-Brahmin confrontations took place in the political arena. The Irish challenge to Brahmin hegemony resulted in bitter conflict. The specter of Irish politics thriving on human weakness and unabashed corruption haunted the city's proper Bostonians. The pragmatic and earthy kinds of politics embraced by Boston's Irish politicians stood in sharp contrast to the idealized Brahmin outlook of disinterested public service.[9] "Political corruption in the city is a principal evil because it spreads like a contagious disease to all sections of the city" warned Robert A. Woods, Boston's foremost social reformer.[10] Consequently, Brahmin stereotypes of the Irish generated "an image of intimate, painful proportions.... The lowly peasant from the Emerald Isle was ignorant, shiftless, credulous, impulsive, mechanically inept, and boastful of the Old Country. The inclination toward drinking and related crimes, elsewhere emphasized with humor, induced gloomy deprecations in New England."[11]

The intensity of Brahmin antipathy toward Boston's Irish citizens revealed much about Brahmin culture at the turn of the century. Like Charles Francis Adams, Jr.'s retreat from Quincy, Brahmins generally rejected the democratic principles of their forefathers. They chose instead "to think of themselves as an aristocratic elite rooted in the country, after the English model." As new and more threatening immigrant groups poured into Boston, the Brahmins increasingly "recoiled in despair from what the nation and the city had become."[12] "The story of immigration into Boston for the last twenty years is for the most part an influx of Jews and Italians followed by more Jews and Italians," Frederick A. Bushee bluntly stated in 1902.[13] The solution that most Brahmins sought to the problems created by the influx of Jewish and Italian immigrants was the elimination of free immigration to the United States. The bitter antagonisms generated between Irish and Brahmins in politics spilled over into socioeconomic and cultural realms. The problems created by new waves of immigrants frequently threatened to overwhelm Boston's Brahmin community. Robert A. Woods summarized the situation:

> But a final overwhelming incursion of helpless, inarticulate foreigners swept in upon the North End, and in less degree upon the West End, necessarily postponing the larger growth of personal philanthropy, and precipitating sanitary, industrial and moral problems so threatening that it became necessary to call upon the State for new and unprecedented forms of legislative action.[14]

Stereotypes of Italians and Jews worsened as the rise of Italian and Jewish immigrants skyrocketed in Boston between 1875 and 1920. The 1875 Census of Massachusetts listed 2,389 Italian residents of Boston. In 1910 the number reached 49,753. Between 1910 and 1920 the city's Italian community grew by over 27,000 individuals. The rapid influx of Jewish immigrants from Eastern Europe, principally Russian, equally dismayed the city's Brahmin elite. In 1875 Russian Jews numbered around 430 individuals. In

1910 immigrants from Russia numbered 64,238. By 1920 Boston's Jewish community included over 85,000 members. From a citywide perspective, the dramatic increase of first- and second-generation immigrants constituted a distressing picture to Boston's embattled Brahmins. In 1875 Irish immigrants made up 20.41 percent of the city's total population.[15] In 1920 the Irish comprised 31.90 percent of Boston's population and the Hub's Jewish and Italian communities constituted 15.70 percent and 14.00 percent of the city's population. In terms of the total percentage of foreign white stock (first- and second-generation immigrants) Boston ranked second only to New York City with a staggering 71.50 percent.[16]

Brahmins distinguished between Northern and Southern Italians from the very beginning of the Southern Italian invasion of Boston in the 1880's. Consequently, Brahmins viewed those Italians from Northern Italy as a part of Western civilization. Their Germanic blood and artistic achievements sharply distinguished them from the ignorant peasants of Southern Italy.[17] The tendency of Southern Italian immigrants to return to Italy and their cultural and physical isolation from Boston's Yankee culture made them particularly unsuitable American citizens.[18] But even more disturbing images evolved as the city's Southern Italian population swelled to nearly one hundred thousand members in the twentieth century. The larger percentage of males to females and their excessive crowding in tenements bred a predisposition toward crime. "Being an excitable race, the Italians resort to knives and pistols over cards or from jealousies arising from the relationship of the sexes."[19] "...the notion grew that the Southern Italian, with his ancient stiletto and his newly adopted revolver, had an innate, spontaneous capacity for violence, which might at any moment culminate a quarrel or feud with murder."[20]

Brahmin views of Jewish immigrants were perhaps the most complex of all immigrant stereotypes.[21] Initially, Brahmins perceived Jews with admiration, seeing in their ancient heritage "the fountainhead of Christianity, inherited from the seventeeth-century Puritans." A second perspective emphasized "guilt and sympathy for the persecuted Jew stimulated by the philosophy of humanitarianism in the nineteenth century." But the third "New England" stereotype of the Jew, stimulated by the arrival of Russian Jews during the 1880s, was distinctly xenophobic. By 1900 images of the physical degeneracy and moral depravity of Russian Jews abounded in Brahmin Boston. "Rarely drunk but very prone to mental diseases, he lived by brain rather than by brawn: moreover, he had an inherent dislike for manual and outdoor labor; and it was 'an unalterable characteristic of this peculiar people' to congregate in cities."[22] This perspective dramatically contrasted with "the Yankee's stoic pioneer breed."[23]

As the number of Jewish immigrants rapidly grew in Boston, there were more visible signs of anti-Semitism. In *Americans in Process*, Robert A. Woods's pioneering study of immigrant neighborhoods in Boston's North and West Ends, Frederick A. Bushee justified the Russian persecution of the Jews because of Jewish economic corruption. "The Russian peasant was, of course, no match for the Jew in the instinct for sharp practice in trade. Even hedged in by a multitude of restrictions, the Jews have become an economic power in Russia—too often a grasping and relentless power."[24] Without strict control of Jewish business practices, Jews would come to dominate the Russian economy. The Czar, however, was "unalterably" opposed to Jewish business practices. In assessing the ability of Boston's Irish, Italians, and Jews to adjust to American life, Bushee concluded that "There is sufficient anxiety in the case of each of the racial groups in these districts." His assessment of Boston's immigrant enclaves was indeed gloomy: "...the danger of the situation in the North and West Ends is that a considerable proportion of the newcomers, instead of finding here opportunities of preparation for a more normal life, will be overcome by their own numbers and their isolated situation, and will settle back accepting present conditions as their permanent lot."[25]

It is no coincidence, therefore, that Boston's Brahmin elite sponsored the movement to eliminate free immigration to America throughout the United States. Embattled in Boston by Irish politics and Italian and Jewish slums, Brahmins closed ranks to end the menace posed by European immigrants to American life. In Boston the rising demands for immigrant restriction reflected heightening ethnic tensions in the city. When Prescott F. Hall, Robert de Cour-

cy Ward, and Robert Treat Paine, Jr. founded the Immigrant Restriction League in the 1880s, they represented a minority of
Boston's old stock elite. By 1900, however, the Immigrant Restriction League moved into high gear. Boston's philanthropist Joseph
Lee, the New York publisher Henry Holt, and the influential president of the Massachusetts Institute of Technology Francis A.
Walker joined the league. The attractiveness of immigrant restriction increased for these Brahmin leaders as immigrants poured into
the city between 1900 and 1920. In 1913 financier Henry Lee
Higginson, sponsor of the Boston Symphony Orchestra, joined the
movement. So, too, did Boston's most respected social reformer
Robert A. Woods and the president of Harvard University A.
Lawrence Lowell. In Massachusetts' senior senator, Henry Cabot
Lodge, the Immigrant Restriction League secured its most influential congressional spokesman.[26]

As Brahmin antipathy toward Italians and Jews worsened, support for immigrant restriction fused with the study of eugenics.
"Eugenics transformed the ambitions of Brahmin restrictionists into
a formidable racial ideology."[27] The militant nationalism and
nativism of the war years culminated in the Johnson Act of 1921
and successive laws that drastically reduced the number of immigrants to the United States. Boston's Brahmin elite contributed to
the success of immigrant restriction on a national level and the resurgence of nativism in Boston. In 1922 Harvard Professor Albert
Bushnell Hart and Harvard's President A. Lawrence Lowell supported a plan to restrict the number of Jewish and Negro students at
that university. The actions of Hart and Lowell illustrated the kinds
of alternatives to which many Brahmins turned.[28]

Concern over the threat of immigrants to the quality of American life continued to preoccupy the Brahmins throughout the
1920s. In 1927 A. Lawrence Lowell chaired the committee established to review the Sacco and Vanzetti murder case. Lowell
dismissed any idea that ethnic prejudice played a part in the conviction of the two Italian anarchists.[29] Indeed, Brahmin nativism was a
significant factor in contributing to the salience of Irish, Italian,
and Jewish ethnicity in Boston during the 1920s and 1930s. Despite
rising Irish political power during these years, Brahmin social,
economic, and political power was a key dimension of Boston's

social structure. Consequently, Brahmin nativism and xenophobia strained interethnic relations. The common concern that Irish, Italians, and Jews shared in opposing the virulent nativism of the 1920s tended to mask the estrangement of the Boston Irish from the city's Jewish and Italian residents, however.

Socioeconomic, political, and cultural factors divided Boston's Irish and Italians and Irish and Jews as they continued to separate immigrants and Yankees. In this setting, Boston's Irish, Italians, and Jews struggled to define themselves and their relationships with each other during a period of domestic and international tensions.

SOCIOECONOMIC RELATIONSHIPS

Socioeconomic factors illustrated a number of aspects of ethnicity in Boston between 1880 and 1940. However, Boston was more complex than simply a caste-ridden society comprised of an enormous ethnic proletariat. Stephen Thernstrom destroyed that stereotype in his study of intergenerational mobility in Boston.[30] Thernstrom found that Boston's occupational and economic opportunities were fluid. This was particularly the case for second-generation immigrants who "were noticeably more successful than their fathers in moving into the upper reaches of the occupational structure."[31] Thernstrom found that the Irish middle class in the latter years of the nineteenth century expanded from 10 percent to 38 percent while the number of low manual workers fell from 65 percent to 32 percent. Thernstrom's data standing alone presented a striking picture of a rapidly rising Irish middle class of significant dimensions. But when the occupational adjustments of second-generation Italians, Jews, and British immigrants are compared with those of the Irish, the findings reveal striking differences. Like the Irish, the second-generation Italian middle class increased from 12 percent to 35 percent while the number of manual workers decreased from 65 percent to 38 percent. The British middle class in contrast to Boston's Irish and Italian middle class rose from 26 percent to 53 percent and the number of manual workers fell from 31 percent to 23 percent. Similarly, the East European middle class (principally Jewish) grew from 25 percent to 50 percent while the number of manual workers decreased from 40 percent to 23 percent. Thernstrom concluded that "only the Irish and Italians were drastically overrepresented in jobs at the very bottom of the occupational ladder."[32]

Traditional explanations of immigrant socioeconomic mobility did not account for the dramatic and quite substantial differences in the economic achievements of first- and second-generation Irish, Italians, British, and Jewish immigrants. In particular, the old immigrant-new immigrant thesis was deficient. It suggested that the older immigrant groups—British, German, Scandinavian, and Irish—were easily acculturated to the American political, socioeconomic, and cultural environment. Consequently, their length of residence in the United States and cultural values facilitated rapid socioeconomic mobility. However, in the case of Eastern and Southern European immigrants, it was hypothesized that significant cultural differences and a short length of residence in the United States inhibited acculturation. Thus Northern Europeans possessed characteristics that were more consonant with American culture. "What was thought to be the old-immigrant pattern applied to the British but not to the Irish: What was taken to be the new-immigrant pattern applied to the Italians but not to the East Europeans."[33] In Boston, Irish and Italians floundered on the bottom rungs of the city's socioeconomic ladder. The failure of Irish and Italian mobility is all the more striking because Boston's Jewish community faced intense discrimination along with the Irish and the Italians.[34] Moreover, the assumption that background handicaps, language barriers, peasant origins, and wealth, for example, may have held the new immigrants back is not sufficient to account for the differing rates of upward mobility.[35] The Irish unquestionably possessed significant advantages in language skills, and it would seem that wealth was not a controlling factor because both Eastern European and Italian immigrants were as desperately poor as Irish immigrants.[36] Demographic factors, rates of differential fertility, the size of families, and so on failed to explain differences in achievements since the birth rate for Boston's Irish community was only slightly higher than that of British immigrants and lower than German and Swedish rates. In fact, the Irish had the highest death rate of any group in the city based on a high incidence of infant mortality.[37] The birth rates for Boston's Italians and Jews, in contrast, were the highest in the city.[38]

The striking socioeconomic differences among Boston's Irish, Italians, Jews, and Yankees contributed to a heightened sense of ethnicity during the 1920s and 1930s. The failure of Irish and Italian upward mobility accentuated the cultural differences dividing Irish and Italians from Yankees and Jews and breeding frustration and bitterness. "Virtual apartheid characterized the Boston Chamber of Commerce: not a single important officership by 1929 had been captured by a person with Irish blood."[39] These frustrations were reinforced by Brahmin hegemony in the city's social clubs and corporate boardrooms. For those Irish that had achieved middle-class and upper-class status the hated acronym NINA—"No Irish Need Apply"—was as real in the corporate and social worlds of the 1930s as it had been in the working-class worlds of their immigrant parents and grandparents in the nineteenth century. Mrs. Joseph P. Kennedy, the daughter of John F. "Honey Fitz" Fitzgerald, Boston's irrepressible Irish political leader, noted in her memoirs that bitterness between Irish and Yankees lingered well into the twentieth century. "With the advantages of inherited wealth and status and close-knit interfamily ties, they controlled the banks, insurance companies, the big law firms, the big shipping and mercantile enterprises, and almost all the usual routes to success, and thus were a self-perpetuating aristocracy. They had many admirable qualities. But they were a closed society."[40] In such an environment, Mrs. Kennedy summarized the primary ethnic relationships between Irish and Brahmins: "Between the two groups feelings were, at best, suspicious, and, in general, amounted to a state of chronic antagonism."[41]

But antipathy between Irish and Brahmins marked only the most visible ethnic cleavages in Boston. Tensions between Irish and Italians and Irish and Jews festered as well. Irish hegemony in Boston's labor unions generated conflict. The Irish controlled a near monopoly of elected union positions in the city. Of 347 offices in the city's nonsegregated unions 55 were held by Italians, Jews, French Canadians, or Blacks.[42] "And discounting clothing workers, only twelve percent of union officials were drawn from these four ethnic groups, less than their numerical strength in the total work force would have suggested."[43] In addition, Italian workers frequently encountered discrimination in jobs by the Irish.[44] But it was the social and economic upheaval of the depression that intensified long-standing ethnic cleavages for Boston's Irish, Italians, and Jews.

The years of depression were particularly difficult for those on the lowest rungs of Boston's socioeconomic ladder. The Irish enclaves in South Boston and Charlestown, the Italian-dominated North End and East Boston, the Black neighborhoods of the South End and lower Roxbury, and the newest immigrants from Eastern Europe, especially Poles and Russian Jews who resided throughout the city, bore the brunt of the depression.[45] Economic conditions in the North End were particularly dismal. By 1930, 799 persons per residential acre were crowded together in the North End with the highest percentage of residential density in the city. Boston's 100,000 Italians also claimed one of the city's highest rates of juvenile delinquency. In addition, 35.0 percent of the North End's work force were unemployed. By 1934 that number climbed to a staggering 40.2 percent.[46]

Boston's Irish neighborhoods fared little better than Italian sections. In South Boston, 32.5 percent of its sixty thousand residents were unemployed. Although rates of unemployment in South Boston fell short of the North End's enormous total of 40.2 percent, Irish unemployment was significantly higher than the citywide average of 26.1 percent.[47] The Back Bay and Beacon Hill, Boston's Brahmin stronghold, by contrast, withstood the ravages of the depression better than any other neighborhood. With only 167 persons occupying a residential acre, the Back Bay possessed the lowest rate of juvenile delinquency in the city. During 1934 only 12 percent of the Back Bay's employable men and women were jobless.[48]

Ethnic solidarities increased as a consequence of the economic and social upheavals of the depression years.[49] Initially the resurgence of ethnicity that accompanied the years of economic uncertainty was positive. Ethnicity strengthened pride and self-respect during a traumatic period.[50] But the bitter historic legacies of the past, combined with the socioeconomic tensions of the depression, accentuated differences between groups. This atmosphere contributed to the polarization of Irish, Italian, and Jewish neighborhoods.[51] Like socioeconomic cleavages in general, Boston's political system had long been defined along ethnic lines. The political arena, too, contributed to rising ethnic tensions.

THE POLITICAL SYSTEM

Undoubtedly, the existence of several ethnic groups with distinctive socioeconomic configurations and cultural outlooks helped to define political relations in Boston. The sporadic outburst of Yankee-Brahmin nativism and xenophobia in the nineteenth and twentieth centuries represented one dimension of ethnic politics. But nativism, as a principal illustration of ethnic conflict, was not the exclusive preserve of Brahmin aristocrats or Yankee tradesmen. The Irish reaction to the hordes of arriving Italian and Eastern European immigrants ranged from physical abuse to pragmatic tolerance.[52]

Political rivalries divided Irish and Italians and Irish and Jews as they continued to separate immigrants and Yankees.[53] The pragmatic outlook of Boston's foremost Irish political leaders often masked the estrangement of the Boston Irish from the city's Jewish and Italian communities. When Irish politicians led the fight against the resurgent nativism of the 1920s, their activities were at times both eloquent and convincing. In 1921 Boston's Irish political leadership spoke for all of Boston's immigrants when it appeared likely that Harvard was about to establish formal quotas discriminating against Blacks and Jews.[54] In 1923 the Irish-dominated Knights of Columbus published a monograph series noting the contributions of all ethnic groups to American life. Massachusetts Senator David I. Walsh, Boston's Mayor James Michael Curley, former Mayor John F. Fitzgerald, and Boston's prototypic ward boss Martin Lomasney categorically rejected the xenophobia of the 1920s. In 1928 a campaign poster in James Michael Curley's campaign headquarters captured the essence of this perspective. The poster depicted the Tomb of the Unknown Soldier with the caption: "What a tragedy if we should learn that he was a Jew, Catholic, or Negro."[55]

Yet the principal contributions of Fitzgerald, Lomasney, Curley, and Walsh aimed at justifying the individual Irish American in the eyes of Yankee Boston rather than advancing the interests of all ethnic groups. They ridiculed Boston's Yankee-dominated social structure with relish and thus contributed to the further polarization of the Yankee and Irish communities in twentieth-century Boston. Indeed, Yankee-Irish antagonisms constituted a principal di-

mension of ethnic politics in Boston. Fitzgerald, Lomasney, and
Curley rejected outright the conciliatory posture of nineteenth-century political leaders such as Patrick Collins and P. J. McGuire and
directly challenged Yankee hegemony in city and state politics.

In the nineteenth century, however, the Irish were slow to assert
themselves in politics. The difficult process of building an extensive
network of communal institutions—religious, fraternal, social welfare, economic, and nationalist—diverted energies and resources
away from politics.[56] In this environment, Patrick Collins, P. J.
McGuire, and other Irish politicians preferred to work with Brahmins rather than actively oppose them. For a brief period, the Irish
formed a significant part of the Brahmin-dominated Mugwamp and
Progressive coalitions. But ethnic antagonisms destroyed the
uneasy Irish-Brahmin balance of power. Brahmin support for the
immigrant-restriction movement, a distinctive sense of Anglo-
American *noblesse oblige*, and the rising ethnic assertiveness of the
Irish ultimately inhibited political cooperation. Just as Boston was
closed to outsiders in the economic and corporate realm, Brahmins
feared and resisted the encroaching political power of Boston's
sprawling Irish community.[57]

John F. Fitzgerald's 1909 mayoral victory over Brahmin philanthropist James J. Storrow symbolized the emergence of Irish political power in Boston's municipal government. The Yankee-dominated Massachusetts legislature attempted to limit Irish control in
Boston by imposing external restraints. These frequently took the
form of repeated reorganizations of Boston's city government. In
the wake of Fitzgerald's victory, the Massachusetts legislature re-
organized city council elections on the at-large basis so Yankee
voters in outlying districts would balance Irish strongholds such as
South Boston, Charlestown, Roxbury, and North Dorchester.[58]
Similarly, city elections including mayoral races were made nonpartisan to fragment Irish political solidarities. The Massachusetts
legislature placed the power to appoint Boston's police commissioner and the city's licensing board in the governor's hands to reduce the influence of Boston's Irish mayors.[59] Each year the Massachusetts legislature established Boston's tax limit. This made
Boston the only major city in the United States where taxation was
directed from the state house.[60] Because of Brahmin fears of Irish
political corruption, the Commonwealth of Massachusetts strictly

limited the city's debt. Boston's public debt could not be raised above 2.5 percent of the city's assessed valuations without the permission of the state legislature.[61] As a direct consequence of Fitzgerald's victory, the Massachusetts legislature assumed control over the Boston Financial Commission (the Fin. Com.). The Fin. Com. became a powerful weapon of Yankee Republicans because it possessed the power to subpoena witnesses and launch investigations of Irish Democrats.[62]

It was in this atmosphere of mutual suspicions and ethnic antagonisms that James Michael Curley became the most visible political spokesman for a militant Irish ethnic outlook. When he spoke of "Back Bay Bourbons" or proclaimed that the term "codfish Aristocracy was a reflection upon the fish," his sense of humor was devastating and he made his point. Moreover, when he recalled with considerable feeling that "even as a boy I knew I belonged to an Irish Catholic minority who were despised socially and discriminated against politically," Curley openly expressed long-suppressed ethnic frustrations.[63] Throughout his fifty years in Boston politics, Curley served as "the idol of a cult, arbiter of a social clique, and spokesman for a state of mind."[64] Political conflict between Brahmins and Irish formed one of Boston's principal ethnic divisions throughout the 1920s and 1930s. But political antagonisms also tended to separate Irish and Jews and Irish and Italians as well.

Just as the Yankee-dominated Massachusetts legislature attempted to counterbalance Irish political strength in Boston politics, the Boston Irish exerted near monopoly control over the workings of Boston's city government. By 1920 the Irish had transformed the city's bureaucracy into an elaborate political fiefdom. The police and fire departments, water and public works, and the school department all had strong Irish representation. An extensive patronage system hailed the ascendancy of Irish politics. Above all, the Boston Irish were overrepresented in elective offices. The school committee was an Irish bastion of power.[65] The Boston City Council was overwhelmingly Irish as well. Of the 110 elected city councilmen between 1924 and 1949 there were only 12 Jews, 9 Yankees, 4 Italians, and 1 Black. All the remaining councilors were Irish.[66] Unquestionably, Irish control of Boston's political process alienated substantial numbers of Jews and frustrated many Italians throughout the 1920s and the 1930s. Ward voting patterns between

1928 and 1940 revealed important differences between Irish, Italians, Jews, and Yankees.[67] The Irish of South Boston supported the Irish-dominated Democratic party more intensely than any other ethnic group in Boston. Irish support ranged from a high of 87 percent in 1928 to a low of 77 percent in 1940. Boston's Italian community also supported Massachusetts' Irish Democrats. Support for the Democratic party in Boston's most heavily Italian wards ranged from 80 percent in 1928 to a low of 66 percent in 1940. The most striking differences among Boston's non-British immigrant groups arose between Irish and Jews. With the exception of the elections of 1934 and 1936, the darkest period of the depression in Boston, Irish Democrats barely received 50 percent of the city's Jewish vote. Similarly, Boston's Brahmin stronghold, Ward 5—the Back Bay and Beacon Hill—overwhelmingly rejected Irish political leadership.[68]

Ethnic differences characterized the political organization of Boston's Irish, Italians, and Jews on the ward level. The Democratic party in Jewish Ward 14 was a closed Irish political club. It was only through the Republican party that Jews could become involved in city politics on a local level. Consequently, support for the Republican party persisted in Dorchester's heavily Jewish neighborhoods throughout the 1920s and 1930s. In 1928, 78 percent of Ward 14's Jewish voters were Republican. In 1932 all of the Republican state committeemen in Ward 14 were Jewish while all of their Democratic counterparts were Irish. As late as 1936, eight of the ten Jews elected to the Massachusetts General Court throughout the state were Republicans.[69] "All of these factors—vestigial Republican affiliations, the anti-Tammany and anti-Irish traditions, the reform tradition and the liberalism and internationalism of the Jews—often caused Jewish dissatisfaction with Democrats on the state and local level. . . ."[70]

Political differences also separated Irish and Italians. Although Boston's Italian community consistently voted Democratic throughout the 1920s and 1930s, internal regional and cultural divisions and gerrymandered districts destroyed Italian political power. Irish politicians managed to represent overwhelmingly Italian constituencies in Wards 1 and 3. By 1930 not a single Italian had been elected to the city council or the state legislature. Throughout the

1920s and 1930s Boston's Italians unsuccessfully battled with their
Irish political overlords. It was only with Joseph Russo's election to
the Boston City Council in 1939 that the Hub's Italians made any
real political advancements.[71]

CULTURAL CLEAVAGES

Distinctive cultural values were expressed in different ways in the
city's Irish, Italian, and Jewish communities. In Boston's Jewish
neighborhoods, distinctive cultural traditions found expression in
patterns of upward socioeconomic mobility.[72] A community of
well over seventy-five thousand individuals was not monolithic in
any sense, however. Boston's Jewish community was characterized
by a dizzying panoply of communal institutions ranging from the
sixteen community organizations sponsored by the Associated Jewish Philanthropies to the Hecht Neighborhood House, the Anti-
Defamation League of B'nai B'rith, the American Jewish Congress,
the American Jewish Committee, the World Zionist Organization,
and the widely respected *Jewish Advocate*. Cultural differences between Boston's small community of German Jews and its larger
numbers of East European (Russian) Jews added religious divisions
to economic ones in the early years of the twentieth century. By
1936, however, the greater part of Boston's Jewish community had
settled in the working-class and lower-middle-class neighborhoods
of Roxbury, Dorchester, and Mattapan. Thus the exodus of Jews
from the immigrant slums and ghettos of the West End to Dorchester and Mattapan lessened the social and economic differences
that tended to divide Boston's Jewry at the turn of the century. The
enlightened director of the Hecht Neighborhood House, which
moved to Dorchester from the West End in 1935, recorded this
changing outlook: "In the West End we were a settlement house
with Jewishness only a secondary consideration. In Dorchester we
are a Jewish Community Center, accepting the philosophy of the
Jewish Center Movement—to provide a place where all ages and
both sexes of Jews may be adjusted as Jews to the American
scene."[73]

Similarly, a number of Jews gained entrance into Boston's social
welfare circles. The Jewish community contributed several out-

standing members of the Consumer's League, the Women's Educational and Industrial League, the Boston Housing Authority, and the National Association for the Advancement of Colored People (NAACP). Mrs. Arthur Rotch and Margaret Weisman were influential members of the Consumer's League. Lois Rantoul represented Boston's Jewry as a director of the Women's Trade Union League. David K. Niles worked with Boston's liberal establishment as an important member of the NAACP and through his involvement with the Ford Hall Forum. The Ford Hall Forum brought a wide-ranging speakers series to Boston representing every shade of opinion. In Louis Kirstein, one of Boston's leading merchants, the Jewish community possessed a superb fund raiser of national import. In Professor Felix Frankfurter of the Harvard University Law School and Supreme Court Justice Louis D. Brandeis, Boston's Jewry contributed two of the nation's foremost legal scholars. In Boston's rabbinates and through the extraordinary publishership of Alexander and Joseph Brin's *Jewish Advocate*, Boston's Jewish community embraced a liberalism and urbanism that stood in contrast to the cultural outlooks of Boston's Italian and Irish neighborhoods.[74]

Unlike the historic isolation and defensiveness of Irish South Boston and the cultural alienation of the Italian North End and East Boston, Boston's Jewish community epitomized cultural values that facilitated integration with the city's Brahmin elite, at least in political, social welfare, and social areas. The rapid upward socioeconomic mobility of Boston's Jews in educational achievements, the professions and business, and, consequently, social status was an essential condition of their entrance into circles that had been closed to all immigrants and their children. But wealth was not the only prerequisite for acceptance in Boston's Brahmin and Yankee circles as the Joseph P. Kennedys and other wealthy Irish families understood so well. The cultural values of many middle-class and upper-class Jews—a political liberalism, social welfare concerns, commitment to the arts—constituted an entree into some of Boston's most exclusive clubs and organizations. Indeed, Jewish cultural values eased the journey, often taking only two generations, from the immigrant ghettos of the West End or the working-class neighborhoods of Roxbury and Mattapan to the affluence of Brookline, Newton, and Wellesley. It was at times a difficult journey but it was accomplished with remarkable speed.

Distinctive cultural values provided insight into the dynamics of ethnicity in Italian East Boston, the North End, and the West End during the 1920s and 1930s. Indeed, cultural values helped to retard upward socioeconomic mobility for Boston's Italian community. Initially, the agrarian background of the majority of Boston's Italians undervalued the importance of occupational mobility. Later, Italian reliance on neighborhood institutions, family ties, and the peer group limited occupational and educational achievement.[75]

But distinctive cultural values influenced the development of Boston's Italian community in a number of other areas. First, Italian emphasis on the family, neighborhood, and peer group tended to isolate the North End, West End, and East Boston from the outside world. Irish political discrimination and Brahmin-Yankee socioeconomic prejudice reinforced these parochial tendencies in Italian Boston. Second, the marked stability of Italian neighborhoods in the North End and East Boston acted as barriers to the outside world. Surrounding the Old North Church and other colonial landmarks, the Italian North End was a popular tourist attraction—which served to accentuate its cultural distinctiveness from the rest of Boston. Third, divisions within Italian Boston based on regional and family ties factionalized the community. In both the nineteenth and twentieth centuries, the North End resembled a patchwork of conflicting cultural, regional, and familial subdivisions. The lack of unanimity within the community diverted attention away from the outside world.[76]

Political, socioeconomic, and cultural isolation bred resentment and bitterness in many of Boston's Italian neighborhoods.[77] Italian-Irish antagonisms resulted in sporadic ethnic conflict between Italian and Irish gangs in the nineteenth and twentieth centuries. Irish residents of East Boston and the North End resisted the massive waves of Italian immigrants between 1880 and 1900 with fierce determination. Although the majority of the Irish residents of the North End had retreated to Charlestown, South Boston, and

Roxbury by the turn of the century, Irish gangs continued to control the waterfront area of the North End at night. After dark, it was unsafe for Italians, Jews, or Negroes to walk along the dock areas. Irish control of the North End's waterfront enraged the growing number of Sicilian fishermen resulting in frequent confrontations. Gang fights between Italians and Irish took place regularly near Italian and Irish neighborhoods in the 1920s and fights between Italians and Irish often broke out after football games in the 1930s.[78] But Italian-Irish ethnic conflict was only one illustration of the intense cultural cleavages that separated Boston's Italian community from the city as a whole. Political, religious, and economic institutions actively discriminated against Italians.

Irish control of Boston's government and bureaucracy, ethnic conflict in the administration of the church, and Italian-Irish economic competition reinforced a sense of isolation and bitterness in Italian Boston.[79] Moreover, Italians rallied against Brahmin economic discrimination and ethnic prejudice although Italian and Yankee contacts were seldom, if ever, violent. Not a single Brahmin-supported settlement house in the North End or the West End had a professional social worker who could speak Italian until 1940. Similarly, every professional social worker in the North or West Ends was Yankee save one Italian.[80] Political, socioeconomic, and cultural factors tended to isolate Boston's Italian community from the rest of the city. In this respect, its significant ethnic press, *La Notizia*, *Gazzetta del Massachusetts*, and the *Italian News* frequently played upon communitywide feelings of bitterness and isolation.[81] One resident of the West End probably best summarized the sense of alienation and cultural isolation experienced by many Italians in Boston during the latter years of the 1930s:

> You don't know how it feels to grow up in a district like this. You go to the first grade—Miss O'Rourke. Second grade—Miss Casey. Third grade—Miss Chalmers. Fourth grade—Miss Mooney. And so on. At the fire station it is the same. None of them are Italians. The police lieutenant is an Italian, and there are a couple of Italian sergeants, but they have never made an Italian captain in the North End. In the settlement houses, none of the people with authority are Italians.[82]

Distinctive cultural outlooks characterized Boston's Irish enclaves of South Boston, Charlestown, and Roxbury as well. Indeed
Oscar Handlin's study of ethnic conflict in nineteenth-century Boston documented the political, socioeconomic, and cultural gulfs
that separated the city's Irish and Brahmin communities. The arrival of Italian and Jewish immigrants in late nineteenth-century
Boston complicated the role played by the city's Irish community.
On one hand, the Irish might have built a formidable ethnic alli-
ance among Italians and Jews as Irish Democrats did in New York
City and Chicago.[83] The Irish were Boston's oldest non-British immigrant group. Between 1900 and 1910, the Irish captured the
Hub's Democratic party, dominated the city's unfolding labor
movement, and controlled the city's government. With a genius for
political organization and an affinity for direct political participation, the Irish were the logical leaders of Boston's "newer races."
But the Irish never successfully built political bridges to Boston's
Italian and Jewish communities. The Jews retained strong Republican affiliations throughout the 1920s while the Italians grudgingly
gave their votes to Irish politicians. Martin Lomasney's career in
Boston politics exemplified these political and ethnic relationships.
Lomasney, Boston's prototypic Irish boss, managed to maintain
political power in Boston's Italian and Jewish neighborhoods
through cleverly gerrymandered districts, fraud, and a low rate of
Italian and Jewish voter participation. The Irish monopoly of
power in Boston alienated Jewish and Italian voters while it further
exacerbated ethnic differences among these groups.[84]

On the other hand, the Boston Irish might have formed a coalition
with liberal Brahmins to implement progressive legislation benefiting
all of Boston's newcomers. Indeed, P. J. McGuire, Patrick Collins,
and Archbishop John Williams consistently worked with Brahmins
in the late nineteenth century to secure these ends.[85] A rising tide of
Irish ethnic militance and a heightening Brahmin xenophobia in the
first decades of the twentieth century destroyed any attempt at
cooperation, however.

Both alternatives were unrealistic in Boston because of the sali-
ence of ethnicity that separated the Boston Irish from the city's
Italians, Jews, and WASPS. In politics, the sheer size of Boston's
Irish population assured them political control of city government.

But political power did not confer social status or economic mobility. In these two respects, the Irish fared little better than the Italians and much worse than the Jews. Indeed, the Irish lack of socioeconomic mobility reinforced a sense of bitterness and failure in South Boston, Charlestown, and Roxbury. The Irish were no longer illiterate immigrants but they were not achieving middle-class status either. Many members of Boston's Irish community lived in a kind of limbo—distinct from the city's Italians and Jews by virtue of their length of residence in Boston— but unlike the city's Brahmins and Yankees in social status and occupational mobility. Italians and Jews saw the Irish as the first Americans they encountered in Boston. From a Brahmin perspective, however, the Irish were American by birth but not quite American in cultural attributes. Undoubtedly, an Irish desire for increasing socioeconomic mobility in view of their objective socioeconomic position explained a great deal about Irish resentment and bitterness.[86]

Contemporary observers in Boston noted the Irish dilemma— neither immigrant nor respected citizen. In *Americans in Process* and the *City Wilderness*, Robert A. Woods and his team of social workers speculated on the reasons why the Irish failed to achieve rapid upward mobility in Boston.[87] In *The Zone of Emergence*, Robert A. Woods and Albert Kennedy analyzed the problems facing the second- and third-generation immigrants of South Boston, Roxbury, Charlestown, and Dorchester. As Woods and Kennedy noted: "The Irish dominate, indeed, the zone of emergence is the great Irish belt of the city." The most striking feature of the zone of emergence was its pervasive mood of monotonousness and drabness. "These were not the packed slums of Boston's North End or New York City, but rather the small drab section of little two- and three-story houses and barracks such as could be found in any New England mill town."[88]

In this atmosphere of physical drabness and cultural ambivalence an Irish ethnic outlook developed in the twentieth century. The rhetoric of politicians like John F. Fitzgerald, Martin Lomasney, and James Michael Curley exemplified this outlook. Throughout his turbulent career in Boston politics, Curley was as much a tribal chieftain as a political leader.[89] As one student of Boston politics described him: "Perhaps above all he understood that the needs of the people had changed; no longer illiterate immigrants, they wanted parks, playgrounds, schools, beaches and hospitals rather than food and loads of coal."[90] But the Boston Irish demanded more than socioeconomic mobility; their depressed socioeconomic status heightened their desire for respectability in Boston. Indeed, James Michael Curley's career in Boston politics illustrated the extent to which ethnic frustrations permeated the city's Irish neighborhoods, particularly in South Boston, Charlestown, and Roxbury.

Irish frustrations over real and imagined socioeconomic injustices extended to other communal institutions as well. In Irish Boston no other institution exerted as much power as that of the Roman Catholic church and its influential archbishop, William Cardinal O'Connell. O'Connell single-handedly dominated the church in Boston. The cardinal infused his administration of the archdiocese with a strident ethnic consciousness like his political counterparts. The ethnic slurs of O'Connell's boyhood in the Yankee-dominated mill town of Lowell, Massachusetts, remained with him for the rest of his life. "As I look back upon my earliest days at school, I can only regard them as a severe drill and without the slightest feeling of enjoyment; with only the full apprehension that without any excuse at all we Catholic boys would be made to understand our inferiority to the other children, blessed with the prop of Protestant inheritance and English or Puritan blood."[91] But even more important than his own self-perceptions of past ethnic injustices, O'Connell challenged the largely conciliatory outlook of his ecclesiastical predecessor with a relentless determination "to idealize and justify the Irish American."[92] Essentially, the thrust of O'Connell's administration was to make respectable the individual Irish American in the eyes of Brahmin Boston. He accomplished this through a complex and autocratic ecclesiastical organization having influence on all segments of the diocese and overseeing all dimensions of its life. In fact, Woods and Kennedy saw the influence of the church as one of the few positive features of the drab zone of emergence: "Their exceptionally adequate and strategically located churches; their parochial schools capable of caring for practically all the girls and many of the boys; their sodalities, societies, and boys clubs; and their possession of a fairly well defined and powerful community sentiment; gives them a singularly complete communal life of their own."[93]

O'Connell's work in building an enormous parochial school system was illustrative of his influence in Boston's Irish community. Between 1922 and 1940 the number of parishes that maintained elementary schools doubled from 76 to 158; the number of high schools tripled from 22 to 67; and the number of pupils increased from 48,172 to 90,576.[94] Moreover, O'Connell brought a host of fraternal, social, and welfare organizations under his explicit direction. In 1908 the archdiocese assumed control of the *Boston Pilot*, Boston's oldest Irish newspaper. Thus O'Connell acquired an important vehicle from which to further direct members of the Archdiocese of Boston.[95] Although O'Connell hardly spoke for every Irish Catholic, he exerted great influence on the Boston Irish.[96]

James Michael Curley and William Cardinal O'Connell expressed many of the same ethnic frustrations in vastly different ways. Both Curley and O'Connell shared a cognizance of ethnic injustices. Each man sought respect as well as power. In their understanding of the importance of ethnic bonds, both O'Connell and Curley demonstrated the potency of ethnic ties for the Boston Irish. Rose Fitzgerald Kennedy, writing of her young adulthood in Boston, also pointed to ethnicity as a fundamental aspect of life in twentieth-century Boston:

> With such "cultural lags," still widespread then [1910] in Boston, I suppose it was inevitable and even in some atavistic way "natural" that there would be two societies. And so there were. Separate "society columns" were published in the newspapers, one about them, one about us.[97]

Mrs. Kennedy's analysis of Boston's social structure illustrated a profound awareness of the salience of ethnicity. In spite of her distinctly upper-class Irish background—growing up in rural Concord, educated in Europe, daughter of the mayor of Boston, financially secure—Mrs. Kennedy nonetheless illustrated the intensity of Irish and Brahmin bitterness. Indeed, the emphasis on "them" and "us" frequently characterized an Irish world view.

The bitter legacy of Irish-Yankee relations manifested itself in "a massive inferiority complex" in Boston's Irish neighborhoods epitomized by South Boston. Thus the Irish found themselves locked into a rigid socioeconomic caste unlike the Irish who immigrated to Chicago or St. Louis. In the West the Irish had "the advantage of growing up with the city." In Boston their working-class status was defined by the "weight" of the past. Thus confrontations between Irish and Brahmins for power and status occurred in each generation. These ethnic cleavages made it exceedingly difficult for any meaningful Irish advancement aside from the political arena.[98]

Ethnic differences were not only expressed in antagonisms dividing Irish from Yankees, but laid the basis for the mobilization of collective fears and anxieties against other groups. In South Boston, Charlestown, and Roxbury, it was easy to be against something just because Jews and Italians appeared to favor it.[99] In this setting, cultural cleavages heightened long-standing anxieties and insecurities. These were expressed in animosities ranging from petty jealousies to overt group conflicts.

Thus the cumulative effects of Boston's social structure, cultural cleavages, and socioeconomic tensions among Boston's Irish, Italians, Jews, and Yankees did not augur well for a period of heightening international tensions. Distinctive ethnic outlooks permeated Boston and were reinforced by political, socioeconomic, and cultural differences even though instances of direct ethnic conflict remained muted. The rapidly deteriorating international scene of the 1930s brought to the surface explicit manifestations of ethnic conflict of surprising intensity and alarming proportions. As Sam Bass Warner, Jr. noted:

In the years to come, world wars and depressions would unleash antidemocratic forces that threatened the foundations of the society: its democratic institutions, its property, its ethnic harmony, the chance of each citizen to prosper through capitalist competition. Confronting these challenges stood a metropolitan society physically divided by about forty parochial institutions. So divided, the city denied itself the opportunity to end, through common action against problems, the isolation of its citizens and the fear they held toward each other. So divided, the metropolis was helpless to solve its own problems.[100]

NOTES

1. Robert A. Woods, "Metes and Bounds," in *Americans in Process, A Settlement Study*, ed. Robert A. Woods, (Boston: Houghton, Mifflin & Co., 1902), p. 17; Oscar Handlin, *Boston's Immigrants, A Study in Acculturation*, rev. and enl. ed. (New York: Atheneum, 1970), p. 220.

2. Barbara M. Solomon, *Ancestors and Immigrants, A Changing New England Tradition* (Cambridge: Harvard University Press, 1956), p. 3.

3. Handlin, *Boston's Immigrants*, p. 57.

4. Ibid., p. 88.

5. Ibid., p. 189.

6. Ibid., p. 191.

7. Solomon, *Ancestors and Immigrants*, p. 30.

8. Handlin, *Boston's Immigrants*, p. 184.

9. Robert A. Woods, "Traffic in Citizenship," in *Americans in Process*, ed. Woods, pp. 154-57.

10. Robert A. Woods, "Assimilation: A Two Edge Sword," in *Americans in Process*, ed. Woods, p. 358.

11. Solomon, *Ancestors and Immigrants*, p. 153.

12. Ibid., p. 221.

13. Frederick A. Bushee, "The Invading Host," in *Americans in Process*, ed. Woods, p. 44.

14. Woods, "Metes and Bounds," p. 7.

15. Massachusetts Department of Commerce, *The Census of Massachusetts, 1875: Population and Social Statistics*, vol. 1, pp. 293, 317; and U.S. Department of Commerce, Bureau of the Census, *Fourteenth Census of the United States, 1920: Population*, vol. 2, p. 926.

16. Charles H. Trout, "Boston During the Great Depression 1928-1940" (Ph.D. diss., Columbia University, 1972), p. 37.

17. Solomon, *Ancestors and Immigrants*, p. 164. There were, of course, real differences between Northern Italians and Southern Italians. Northern Italians were better educated; many were artisans, particularly stone cutters; many were irreligious; some of their children became Protestants. Northerns were, by and large, urban. The southerners were primarily agrarian and Catholic. In addition, Northern Italians were literate radicals on the whole. The southerners were semiliterate and conservative. For a penetrating analysis of the Italian American experience, see Richard Gambino, *Blood of My Blood, The Dilemma of Italian Americans* (Garden City, N.Y.: Doubleday, 1975).

18. Bushee, "The Invading Host," pp. 50-51.

19. Ibid., p. 52.

20. Solomon, *Ancestors and Immigrants*, p. 166.

21. Ibid., p. 161.

22. Ibid., p. 164.

23. Ibid., p. 171.

24. Bushee, "The Invading Host," p. 48.

25. Ibid., pp. 49-50, 70.

26. John Higham, *Strangers in the Land, Patterns of American Nativism 1860-1925* (New York: Atheneum, 1974), pp. 141-42; Solomon, *Ancestors and Immigrants*, pp. 123, 124.

27. Ibid., p. 151.

28. J. Joseph Huthmacher, *Massachusetts People and Politics 1919-1933* (Cambridge: Harvard University Press, 1959), pp. 9-16, 93; Solomon, *Ancestors and Immigrants*, pp. 204-5.

29. Solomon, *Ancestors and Immigrants*, p. 205.

30. See, for example, Stephen Thernstrom, *The Other Bostonians, Poverty and Progress in the American Metropolis 1880-1970* (Cambridge: Harvard University Press, 1973), esp. chs. 2, 3, and 4.

31. Ibid., p. 120. Thernstrom's work makes it clear that those second-generation immigrants who entered the middle class tended to cluster "in less attractive and less well paid white collar jobs than Yankees." Nonetheless, Thernstrom concludes that by 1910 the large gulf separating Yankees and first- and second-generation immigrants had narrowed. Ibid., pp. 121-22. The following analysis draws extensively on Thernstrom's work, pp. 136-41.

32. Ibid., p. 140. It should be noted that Thernstrom's data conflict with Andrew M. Greeley's national data for Irish and Italian economic achievements. Greeley finds that Irish and Italians have far outstripped every other group in the United States except Jews in terms of income, prestige, and education. For Greeley's most recent data, see *The American Catholic, A Social Portrait* (New York: Basic Books, 1977).

33. Thernstrom, *The Other Bostonians*, p. 135.

34. Solomon, *Ancestors and Immigrants*, p. 174.

35. Thernstrom, *The Other Bostonians*, p. 163.

36. Ibid., p. 163.

37. Ibid.

38. Ibid.

39. Trout, "Boston During the Great Depression," p. 45.

40. Rose Fitzgerald Kennedy, *Times to Remember* (Garden City, N.Y.: Doubleday, 1974), pp. 50-51.

41. Ibid., p. 51.

42. Trout, "Boston During the Great Depression," p. 46.

43. Ibid.

44. Ibid., p. 40.

45. Ibid., p. 350.

46. Ibid., pp. 40, 351.

47. Ibid.

48. Ibid., pp. 41, 351.

49. Ibid., p. 41.

50. Ibid., p. 525.

51. Ibid.

52. Bushee, "The Invading Host," pp. 61-62; William Foote Whyte, "Race Conflicts in the North End of Boston," *New England Quarterly* 12 (December 1939): 623-42.

53. Lawrence Fuchs, *Political Behavior of American Jews* (Glencoe, Ill.: The Free Press, 1956), p. 58.

54. Huthmacher, *Massachusetts People and Politics*, p. 93.

55. Ibid., pp. 93, 166.

56. See, for example, Handlin, *Boston's Immigrants*; Donna Merwick, *Boston Priests 1848-1910, A Study in Social and Intellectual Change* (Cambridge: Harvard University Press, 1973); Thomas N. Brown, *Irish American Nationalism 1870-1890* (Philadelphia: J.B. Lippincott Co., 1966).

57. Richard M. Abrams, *Conservatism in a Progressive Era, Massachusetts Politics 1900-1912* (Cambridge: Harvard University Press, 1964), p. 147.

58. Edward C. Banfield and James Q. Wilson, *City Politics* (Cambridge: Harvard University Press and M.I.T. Press, 1963), pp. 39, 94-96.

59. Banfield and Wilson, *City Politics*, pp. 94-96.

60. Trout, "Boston During the Great Depression," p. 69.

61. Ibid.

62. Banfield and Wilson, *City Politics*, p. 39; Trout, "Boston During the Great Depression," pp. 70, 71.

63. James Michael Curley, *I'd Do It Again* Englewood Cliffs, N.J.: Prentice-Hall, 1957), pp. 2, 32-33.

64. William V. Shannon, *The American Irish* (New York: Macmillan Co., 1963), p. 209.

65. Boston, Mass.: *Report of the Proceedings of the School Committee of the City of Boston*, June 26, 1939, pp. 136-37.

66. Banfield and Wilson, *City Politics*, p. 95.

67. The data are drawn from gubernatorial elections between 1928 and 1940 in Irish South Boston (Wards 6 and 7); the Italian North End and West End (Ward 3); Jewish Dorchester (Ward 14); and the Yankee Back Bay (Ward 5). Gubernatorial elections were selected because Boston's mayoral elections were nonpartisan, thus blunting ethnic differences. See Boston, Mass.: *Report of the Election Department of the City of Boston, 1928-1940*.

68. Ibid.

69. Fuchs, *Political Behavior of American Jews*, p. 56; *Jewish Advocate*, 10 November 1936.

70. Fuchs, *Political Behavior of American Jews*, p. 56.

71. Walter Firey, *Land Use in Central Boston* (Cambridge: Harvard University Press, 1945), pp. 188-89; Trout, "Boston During the Great Depression," pp. 97, 564; and *Italian News*, 10 November 1939.

72. Jewish socioeconomic mobility exceeded that of every other ethnic group in Boston. Second-generation Jewish immigrants were likely to attend college much more frequently than their Irish or Italian counterparts even though their fathers had less education than first-generation Irish or Italians. The intensity of the Jewish commitment to education emerges not when Jews are compared with Irish or Italians but with British immigrants. Thernstrom notes: "Almost the same fraction of both immigrant groups attained middle-class jobs, and the English immigrants had attended school an average of 2 years more than the Russians. But 44 percent of the second-generation Russian Jews and only 27 percent of their counterparts of English stock attended college, and a corresponding larger fraction of the former found employment in the upper reaches of the middle-class and were in the top income bracket. This seems to be a clear example of the way in which the cultural values of a group can shape the career patterns of its children in a distinctive manner." *The Other Bostonians*, p. 173.

73. "Annual Report of Hecht Neighborhood House, 1939-1940," Papers of Hecht Neighborhood House, American Jewish Historical Society, Waltham, Massachusetts.

74. Trout, "Boston During the Great Depression," p. 53; see also Louis E. Kirstein Papers, Baker Library, Harvard University, Cambridge, Massachusetts; Papers of Hecht Neighborhood House.

75. Stephen Thernstrom's data on Italian socioeconomic mobility, like his findings on Irish mobility, conflict with Andrew M. Greeley's national data. See Thernstrom's *The Other Bostonians*, pp. 174-75, for discussion of the problem.

76. For further documentation of these points, see William F. Whyte, *Street Corner Society, The Social Structure of an Italian Slum* (Chicago: Chicago University Press, 1943), pp. 102-3, 195, 272; Nathan Glazer and Daniel P. Moynihan, *Beyond the Melting Pot*, 2d ed. (Cambridge: M.I.T. Press, 1970), p. 206; Richard Gambino, *Blood of My Blood*, p. 40; Trout, "Boston During the Great Depression," p. 97.

77. Whyte, *Street Corner Society*, p. 195.

78. Bushee, "The Invading Host," pp. 61-62; Whyte, *Street Corner Society*, p. 195; Whyte, "Race Conflicts in The North End of Boston," pp. 613-32, 634-37.

79. Trout, "Boston During the Great Depression," p. 97; Robert H.

Lord, John E. Sexton, and Edward T. Harrington, *History of the Arch-diocese of Boston, In the Various Stages of Its Development 1604-1943*, vol. 3 (New York: Sheed & Ward, 1944), p. 225; Whyte, "Race Conflicts in the North End of Boston," p. 638.

80. Whyte, *Street Corner Society*, pp. 98-99, 102-3, 223. Whyte captured the essence of Italian isolation in Boston when he pointed out that the West End's "...problem is not a lack of organization but the failure of its social organization to mesh with the structure of society around it. This accounts for the development of the local political and racket organizations and also for the loyalty people bear toward their race and toward Italy," p. 273.

81. See chapter 4 for an analysis of Boston's Italian press.

82. Whyte, *Street Corner Society*, p. 216.

83. See, for example, Thomas R. Mason, "Reform Politics in Boston: A Study of Ideology and Social Change in Municipal Government" (Ph.D. diss., Harvard University, 1963), p. 355. Mason finds in the crucial mayoral election of 1909 between John F. Fitzgerald and James J. Storrow that socioeconomic factors were more important than ethnicity.

84. Huthmacher, *Massachusetts People and Politics*, pp. 15-16; Whyte, *Street Corner Society*, p. 211; Trout, "Boston During the Great Depression," p. 97.

85. For a discussion of the conciliatory role of the Catholic Church in nineteenth century Boston, see Merwick, *Boston Priests*, pp. 69-99.

86. Shannon, *The American Irish*, pp. 184-86.

87. See Robert A. Woods, ed., *Americans in Process; A Settlement Study* (Boston: Houghton, Mifflin & Co., 1902); Robert A. Woods, ed., *The City Wilderness* (Boston: Houghton Mifflin & Co., 1898).

88. Robert A. Woods and Albert J. Kennedy, *The Zone of Emergence* (Cambridge: M.I.T. Press, 1962), pp. 36, 135; Sam Bass Warner, Jr., *Streetcar Suburbs, The Process of Growth in Boston 1870-1900* (Cambridge: Harvard University Press and M.I.T. Press, 1962), p. 40.

89. Shannon, *The American Irish*, pp. 202-3.

90. Murray B. Levin, *The Alienated Voter, Politics in Boston* (New York: Holt, Rinehart & Winston, 1960), p. 5.

91. William Cardinal O'Connell, *Recollections of Seventy Years* (Boston: Houghton, Mifflin & Co., 1934), p. 6.

92. Merwick, *Boston Priests*, p. 184.

93. Woods and Kennedy, *The Zone of Emergence*, p. 189.

94. The Archdiocese of Boston experienced a period of remarkable growth under O'Connell's authoritarian guidance. The population of the diocese grew from 750,000 in 1907 to 1,092,078 in 1942, a time when Catholic immigration from Central and Southern Europe ended in the

1920s. The number of parishes rose from 194 to 322 to support the needs of the archdiocese's sprawling population. There was an impressive growth in virtually every aspect of the diocese's life. The number of priests doubled from 488 to 957 during O'Connell's tenure. The number of priests belonging to religious organizations and congregations increased by nearly six-fold—110 to 625. Boston College experienced its "second founding" while O'Connell established two women's colleges, Regis and Emmanuel, and a host of exclusive preparatory academies. In addition, the Diocesan Charitable Bureau, the Society for the Propagation of the Faith, the Legion of Mary, and the Catholic Youth Organization touched the lives of hundreds of thousands of Catholics. Lord, Sexton, and Harrington, *History of the Archdiocese of Boston*, pp. 747-58.

95. Knights of Columbus Papers and Catholic Order of Foresters Papers, Archives of the Archdiocese of Boston, Brighton, Massachusetts. The papers of Knights of Columbus and Catholic Order of Foresters reveal O'Connell's constant involvement in the affairs of the two largest Irish Catholic fraternal orders in Massachusetts; see also Lord, Sexton, Harrington, *History of the Archdiocese of Boston*, pp. 747-55; Merwick, *Boston Priests*, p. 168; O'Connell, *Recollections of Seventy Years*, pp. 294-96.

96. Trout, "Boston During the Great Depression," pp. 55-56, 529-30; Shannon, *The American Irish*, p. 194. Shannon concludes: "For thirty-eight years, from 1906 until his death in 1944 at age eighty-five, Cardinal O'Connell dominated the Catholic scene in Boston. Since the Catholic Church was a formative influence on the Irish, this meant that he did much in a positive and a negative sense, to shape the minds of the Boston Irish."

97. Kennedy, *Times to Remember*, p. 53.

98. Historian Lawrence J. McCaffrey succinctly describes this condition: "Massachusetts Irish Catholics lived in a highly-structured society dominated by a Protestant Ascendancy determined to retain power and the status quo. New England Irishmen started on the basement floor of the American class structure and tended to stay there. Their ghettos were loaded with failure and defeatism, producing a paranoid vision of religion, politics, and other Americans." McCaffrey, *The Irish Diaspora in America* (Bloomington: Indiana University Press, 1976), p. 78-79; Shannon, *The American Irish*, p. 183.

99. Andrew M. Greeley, personal letter, 26 January 1977.

100. Warner, *Streetcar Suburbs*, p. 165.

3

Ethnic Conflict in Boston:
An Irish Perspective, 1935-1939

The worsening international scene of the 1930s constituted an acute identity crisis for the Boston Irish. The force of international events—the specter of communist advances in Mexico and Spain, the Spanish Civil War, the end of American isolation—produced disorientation and confusion in South Boston, Roxbury, and Dorchester. Additionally, the economic hardships of the depression provided fertile ground in which a bitter and defensive Irish outlook flourished.

FATHER CHARLES E. COUGHLIN AND THE BOSTON IRISH: THE DILEMMA OF ETHNICITY IN A CHAOTIC WORLD

In this political, socioeconomic, and psychological atmosphere, past ethnic animosities surfaced while new hostilities emerged. One individual in particular contributed to the shaping of a Boston Irish ethnic outlook during the 1930s—Father Charles E. Coughlin. Father Coughlin, a Catholic priest, enjoyed immense popularity in the Northeast and Middle West during much of the 1930s. His Sunday afternoon radio broadcasts from Royal Oak, Michigan, attracted an audience conservatively estimated at between 20 and 40 million Americans.[1] Father Coughlin gained prominence in 1926 when he took to the airwaves denouncing attempts by the Ku Klux Klan to harass his small parish in suburban Detroit. Father Coughlin was an immensely gifted speaker. His melodious voice and smooth delivery were well suited to radio.

Initially, Father Coughlin's radio broadcasts dealt with religious material. By 1930, however, Coughlin abandoned his religious sermons and turned to contemporary political and economic problems. Foremost in his mind were the economic causes of the depression. He turned to economic explanations but his theories were vague, confused, and erratic. The force of Father Coughlin's deliveries more than made up for their lack of consistency and analytical rigor. "Repetition did not exhaust the attractiveness of the attack, nor did the intellectual confusion in Father Coughlin's presentation undermine its appeal. If the banker is the Devil, can his machinations be denounced and exposed too often?"[2] Coughlin skillfully exploited the fears and frustrations of his listeners. Moreover, the radio priest's rise to national prominence in the early thirties came at a time when there was very little constructive national leadership. Al Smith was becoming more conservative on economic matters but "Franklin Roosevelt had not yet emerged as the spokesman for a distinct point of view." Coughlin manipulated his audience by drawing upon long-standing Populist themes *via* Christian and radical imagery.[3] Coughlin denounced "want in the Midst of Plenty." Over and over again he called upon his listeners to "Drive the Moneychangers from the Temple." He infused his rhetoric with a strident nationalism when he castigated the "British propaganda of the Tory Bankers of lower Manhattan." Coughlin pandered to the fears and prejudices of his audience by endorsing the conspiracy theses then in vogue: "The Merchants of Death" and the greed of the "International Bankers."[4]

The international dimensions of Coughlin's thought were present in the early 1930s although the full depth and intensity of his xenophobia, nationalism, and anti-Semitism did not emerge until after 1936. Coughlin fused domestic socioeconomic anxieties with ill-defined international problems in an ever-increasing upward spiral. Two factors fueled the full articulation of his nativism.

First, in 1935 Coughlin opposed an administration-sponsored protocol providing for American membership in the World Court.

His forceful opposition generally is cited as the principal reason for the triumph of proponents of American isolationism.[5] It seems clear, therefore, that Coughlin's role in defeating American participation in the World Court persuaded him to oppose F.D.R. and the New Deal in a more forceful way.[6] In the spring of 1935, Father Coughlin launched an ill-fated third party, the Union party, in the 1936 election. Apparently the success of his opposition to the World Court and the popularity of his radio broadcasts convinced him that Roosevelt and the New Deal were vulnerable politically. Contrary to his expectations, the Union party polled a miserable 2 percent of the national vote. His humiliating defeat opened the door for more extreme rhetoric. The deteriorating international system, therefore, provided him with the second component of nativism.

Father Coughlin was desperately in need of highly emotional issues to retain his "constituency" and perhaps win back those who deserted him during the 1936 election. Contemporary international events offered the radio priest a golden opportunity to unleash the full fury of his invective. The persecution of the Catholic church in Mexico, the Spanish Civil War, the specter of a worldwide communist assault, the power of international bankers, became his favorite themes. Indeed, as economic conditions in the United States slowly brightened, Father Coughlin reached for emotional topics to sustain his escalating rhetoric and satisfy his demagogic zeal.[7] Over and over again Coughlin inveighed the "internationalism of high finance" and the "internationalism of the merchants of murder."[8] He linked the international bankers to a Jewish conspiracy to take over the world when he published the scurrilous *Protocols of the Elders of Zion* in 1938 and 1939.[9] Moreover, the radio priest saw in the persecution of the Catholic church in Mexico and Spain the triumph of communism, atheism, and Jewish internationalism. These international anxieties, fused with the socioeconomic upheavals of the depression years, reinforced a defensiveness that engendered ethnic conflict and a climate of hate and fear. As the 1930s came to a close, Father Coughlin's frenzied rhetoric increased. The impact of the deteriorating international system was an explicit component of his nativism.[10]

Coughlin's hysterical statements increased. Mussolini was named

"Man of the Week" in the May 16, 1938, issue of *Social Justice*. In the spring of 1940, *Social Justice* proclaimed Mussolini "Man of the Year." Coughlin saw the ubiquitous hand of Jews, internationalists, communists, and atheists in every major international event of the last years of the 1930s.[11] This perspective led him to articulate explicitly anti-Semitism and fascism. From the very beginning of his political broadcasts in the early 1930s, Father Coughlin consistently relied on anti-Semitic innuendos. In fact, his castigation of moneylenders and international financiers—Bernard Baruch, the House of Rothschild, Kuhn and Loeb—foreshadowed his explicit anti-Semitism of 1937-42.[12] By 1937 Coughlin discarded his veiled anti-Semitic attacks on "international bankers." He challenged all Jews to reject the old Hebrew ways of "an eye for an eye and a tooth for a tooth," asking all Jews to act like "good Christians." On a Sunday evening in November 1938, Father Coughlin defended the Nazi persecution of the Jews as a defense mechanism against communism. During a time when Nazi atrocities reached horrendous dimensions in Germany, Coughlin published the *Protocols of the Elders of Zion*. The July 24, 1939, issue of *Social Justice* called the amount of American money spent every year for German Jewish refugees "appalling." Coughlin's anti-Semitism and scapegoating led him to embrace fascism as a political doctrine.[13]

Father Coughlin advocated a "reorganization" of the American government on the basis of a corporatist philosophy. As with most of his practical plans, the "reorganization" of the American government was ambiguous and inconsistent. Italy's corporate form of government served as the model for Coughlin's reorganization proposals. Father Coughlin's fascism involved more than plans to "reorganize" the U.S. government. He organized and supported the formation of the Christian Front platoons in the "expectation" of a communist revolution in the United States. The Christian Front actually was a paramilitary organization equivalent to the Italian Brown Shirts.[14]

In a fundamental sense, Coughlin constituted an intensely complex crisis for American Catholicism and Irish Catholics in particular. In a period of domestic uncertainty only heightened by the international environment, Catholic Americans tried to deal with a series of complex and difficult problems rooted in their political, socioeconomic, and cultural settings. In Boston, where the weight of the city's history tended to accentuate the importance of ethnicity, the search for a meaningful Irish identity erupted into conflict. Father Coughlin and the international environment played significant roles in defining the precise dynamics of that conflict in Boston.

The Boston Irish were among Father Coughlin's most enthusiastic followers. James Michael Curley, an astute observer of Boston politics, described the Hub as the "most Coughlinite city in the United States."[15] When Father Coughlin visited Boston in 1935, he was triumphantly received by the city council and the Massachusetts legislature. At that time, Coughlin maintained that "only Waterloo, Iowa had a higher per capita membership in the National Union of Social Justice [Coughlin's national organization] than Boston."[16] Other sources suggest that South Boston was a prime bastion of support for Father Coughlin during the years of the 1930s.[17] Undoubtedly, there was considerable working-class Irish support for Father Coughlin throughout Massachusetts at least during the early and middle years of the 1930s. In fact, three Democratic congressmen, all representing districts with large working-class Irish constituencies, ran on the Union party ballot in 1936.[18]

When William Cardinal O'Connell rebuked Father Coughlin in 1934 for his radical ideas and irresponsibility, the cardinal received a flood of abusive mail from many members of his archdiocese. Not surprisingly, each letter expressed an intense devotion to Father Coughlin's ideals. Quite aside from their outrage at O'Connell's public criticism of Father Coughlin, there emerged a sense of economic frustration and acute resentment of the cardinal's status, authority, wealth, and influence within the church. These were the men and women whom Coughlin explicitly sought to reach in his weekly radio broadcasts, his newspaper *Social Justice,* and through his personally sponsored organizations—the National Union of Social Justice and the Christian Front. "I have been a member of your church for 57 years," one member of Boston's Irish community wrote to Cardinal O'Connell, "but today I sever all connections with it while you are the head of it here." He continued: "And may I assure you that in Boston today there are thousands of others who feel the same as I do about it. I have come in contact with a great number of our faith in the last two years since this has been going on and have heard nothing but ridicule of you for doing so." Another disgruntled Catholic warned O'Connell: "If you want to get yourself more disliked by the Catholic people of Boston, continue attacking Rev. Father Coughlin. Thousands of people love him, which, I am sorry to say, they do not approve of you." He continued, "Instead of going South This winter with your party and spending Five to Six Thousand Dollars; donate that amount to hundreds of poor families, who are without proper clothing and food; We have long since stop reading the *Pilot* on account of you the way you live ect, while your people starve, you are a fine example...."[19] A more articulate Irish Catholic from Charlestown expressed similar thoughts to his eminence: "Undoubtedly you have lost sight of the fact that you have gravely offended thousands of Roman Catholics by your attack on Father Coughlin. There would be no doubt in your mind if you could be within hearing of the comments."[20]

Father Coughlin exerted great influence in Irish neighborhoods like South Boston and Charlestown precisely because he was able to articulate the bitterness and frustrations that confronted urbanized working-class Irish Catholics during a period when economic considerations and international tensions were of overwhelming importance.[21] The effects of the depression and the deteriorating international system provided a setting in which interethnic tensions increased. Father Coughlin's role, then, was important precisely because it contributed to a climate of opinion conducive to conflict.

The results of the 1936 presidential election illustrated the extent of Father Coughlin's strength in Boston vis-à-vis other American cities. Coughlin's candidates for president and vice-president received more than 5.0 percent of the vote in only four cities: Dubuque, Cincinnati, St. Paul, and Boston. In the Hub, the Union party ran stronger than in any other American city. The Union party captured a full 8.3 percent of the citywide vote in Boston and over 11.0 percent of the vote in the Irish working-class neighborhoods of South Boston and Charlestown. In Jewish Ward 14, the Union party received only 2.5 percent of the vote.[22]

The role of Coughlinite candidates for offices other than presi-

dent and vice-president also illustrated Father Coughlin's residual
strength in Boston. Congressman John W. McCormack, whose district included South Boston, Roxbury, and Dorchester, faced one
of the stiffest fights in his very successful political career.
Throughout the 1930s, McCormack, in contrast to many other
Irish politicians, vigorously rejected the militant isolationism and
Anglophobia that Father Coughlin skillfully manipulated. The
1936 electoral returns accorded McCormack's opponent, Albert P.
McCulloch (Coughlin's endorsed candidate), an unprecedented
31.2 percent of the vote. Similarly, James Michael Curley felt the
sting of Irish support for Father Coughlin. Curley was narrowly
defeated in a race for the United States Senate by the young Henry
Cabot Lodge, III, because Coughlin's candidate for the U.S. Senate
received over 37,000 votes that probably would have gone to
Curley.[23]

But ethnic conflict in Boston transcended the ballot box, as
Coughlin's preoccupation with international events after 1937 intensified. Father Coughlin exacerbated preexisting ethnic tensions
in South Boston, Charlestown, and Dorchester as he did in
Brooklyn, the Bronx, and Queens, New York. The radio priest introduced a climate of hate, bitterness, and discord in Irish enclaves
where frustrations, failure, and defeatism had been fermenting for
a generation, thus serving as a prime catalyst for the outbreak of
ethnic conflict. Irish gang attacks occurred on Jewish youths near
Jewish neighborhoods in Roxbury and Dorchester in the mid and
latter 1930s—the years of Coughlin's most vocal and intense anti-
Semitism. In addition, Coughlin's fascist oganizations flourished in
Boston and New York.[24] Francis P. Moran, a longtime disciple of
Coughlin, served as leader of the Christian Front in Boston. Moran
contributed articles to *Social Justice* reporting how Jews attacked
newsboys selling *Social Justice* on the streets of Boston.[25]

The hard-core supporters of the Christian Front probably represented a small number of socially maladjusted and desperate individuals. Nonetheless, their extremist activities served to heighten
ethnic tensions and legitimize more subtle anti-Semitic stereotypes
within the larger Irish community. Thus the Irish of South Boston,
Charlestown, Roxbury, and Dorchester sullenly perceived the economic and social mobility of Boston's Jews.[26] Father Coughlin,

therefore, intensified stereotypes of Jewish economic influence but demographic factors in Boston also played a significant role in generating ethnic conflict. The exodus of Jews from the immigrant ghettos and slums of Boston's West End into Irish neighborhoods in Dorchester, Roxbury, and Mattapan began in the 1920s. By the mid 1930s a large Jewish enclave had displaced Irish neighborhoods, particularly along Mattapan's Blue Hill Avenue. Coughlin's anti-Semitism, complex international events, and heightened Irish-Jewish tensions in Boston reinforced Irish frustrations over their lack of socioeconomic success. The majority of Boston's Irish played no part in Coughlin's fascist organizations or attacked Jews verbally or physically, but tensions between the Irish and Jewish communities nonetheless increased. The salience of the international environment contributed to a strikingly defensive and strident Irish outlook in the latter years of the 1930s. Father Coughlin played an important role in these circumstances but he hardly acted alone. Boston's influential Irish church and political leaders contributed to the outbreak of ethnic conflict in Boston.

IRISH CATHOLICISM AND THE INTERNATIONAL ENVIRONMENT: THE CATHOLIC CHURCH AND ETHNIC CONFLICT IN BOSTON

William Cardinal O'Connell, the imposing archbishop of Boston, exerted great influence on Boston's Irish community.[27] During a period of domestic social changes and international instability, the church remained a stable cultural and ethnic institution for the Boston Irish. As the dean of the American hierarchy, O'Connell was among the most visible Catholic churchmen in the country. As such he received information, requests for financial assistance, and visitors from all over the world.[28] Thus the cardinal's autocratic temperament and powerful status in the American church gave him a unique vantage point to evaluate the contemporary international system. His eminence used every means at his disposal to publicize his views of international issues.

Cardinal O'Connell despised Father Coughlin personally and unequivocally rejected Coughlin's racism and anti-Semitism. As early as April 1932, the cardinal denounced Coughlin's political and economic activism. O'Connell's initial attack was followed up in December 1934 and again that same winter.[29] On March 28, 1936, the *Boston Pilot* noted: "There is, first of all, the compelling disability imposed by truth. The liar possesses no right of free speech which would permit him as an errant fancy might please to culminate other men and institutions. . . . The liar has no right to express his lie."[30] Unlike the radio priest, Cardinal O'Connell did not turn a deaf ear to the Nazi persecution of the Jews in Germany. The cardinal consistently condemned the persecution of both Jews and Catholics under the Nazi reign of terror. When Father Coughlin published the *Protocols of the Elders of Zion*, Father Michael J. Ahern, S.J., speaking for the Archdiocese of Boston, denounced them as trash in his popular weekly radio commentary and in the *Boston Pilot*.[31]

Despite Cardinal O'Connell's undisguised contempt for all that Father Coughlin represented, agreement on three main contemporary international issues masked their differences. These issues included: the threat of communist expansion, the persecution of the Catholic church in Mexico and Spain, and support for American isolationism. As the international system worsened in the final years of the 1930s, Cardinal O'Connell, his priests, and the *Boston Pilot* embraced a shrill defensiveness that strained relationships with Boston's Jews and liberal Protestants. The force of the international system provided a frame of reference in which explicitly ethnic antagonisms emerged in Boston's Irish neighborhoods.[32]

The deteriorating international climate heightened the differences between Catholic and non-Catholic communities in the United States. These differences became even more pronounced in Boston where ethnic antagonisms had intensified throughout the 1930s. Thus international events played an increasingly important role in exacerbating already strained ethnic relationships in Boston. Unquestionably, American foreign policy fostered Irish Catholic "disenchantment" with the international and domestic initiatives of the Roosevelt administration. Catholic persecution in Mexico and American recognition of the Soviet Union "as well as the prominence of such allegedly leftist advisors as Rexford Tugwell, Harry Hopkins, and Felix Frankfurter" created problems for Irish Catholics generally.[33] In Boston, James Michael Curley asked Jim

Farley to "keep New Dealers like Rexford Tugwell, Frances Perkins, and Felix Frankfurter out of Boston. The opinion of most persons is that they are communistic." William Cardinal O'Connell wholeheartedly agreed. In a radio address to the nation on July 4, 1934, his eminence denounced those who "will dictate to us even against our will... [and] will rule us as if they had a divine right to rule. That is autocracy."[34] Cardinal O'Connell's antipathy to the New Deal and strident ethnic defensiveness only heightened as the importance of international events increased.

Indeed, the *Boston Pilot* saw in the threat of atheistic communism the single greatest menace to world peace and domestic harmony. Throughout the decade, prominent priests of the archdiocese spoke out against the menace of communism. The Very Reverend Louis J. Gallagher, S. J., president of Boston College, decried the "brutality, inhumanity, and degradation" of communism. Even the more liberal Rev. Jones I. Corrigan, S.J., professor of economics at Boston College, was not above noting the ubiquitous threat posed by communists in the armed forces, labor organizations, and American school systems. The *Boston Pilot* perhaps expressed best the linkages between American domestic and foreign policies when it concluded that U.S. recognition of the Soviet Union strengthened the forces of worldwide communism. Indeed, the aims of communism—the abolition of religion, the degradation of mankind, and the overthrow of American democracy—presented an intolerable threat to Boston's Irish Catholics. The *Pilot* succinctly stated this perspective when it noted that "Communism is the major evil of our time."[35]

Given the parameters of such an ideological and cultural outlook, the specter of Catholic persecution in Mexico and Spain only confirmed the imminence of communist subversion throughout the world. In each case, the perceptions of American Catholics frequently conflicted sharply with the perceptions of liberal Protestants and Jews. Boston's Irish Catholics grimly watched the persecution of the church in Mexico. The revolution in Mexico, like the Spanish Civil War, presented Boston's Irish with immensely powerful emotional issues.[36]

The refusal of Jews and Protestants to condemn the savagery of Catholic persecution in Mexico outraged the *Pilot*. In 1935 it rancorously complained that the American press objected more "to the brief Hitler regime" than to the sustained and brutal persecution of the church in Mexico.[37] An Irish sense of bitterness and frustration over perceived second-class citizenship—a key dimension of a Boston Irish outlook—pervaded such frustrations. Cardinal O'Connell effectively exploited Irish Catholic defensiveness. In a letter read at all the masses in the Archdiocese of Boston on Sunday, June 1, 1935, the cardinal declared: "An atheistic minority has seized control of that great Catholic nation and has sought by armed force to impose upon the Mexican people a denial of everything which it has held sacred for years."[38]

The Spanish Civil War only reinforced the imminence of worldwide communist subversion and the cultural gulf separating Boston's Irish Catholics and liberal Protestants and Jews. In Boston the *Pilot's* coverage of events in Spain was comprehensive and, at times, sensational. The *Pilot* printed stories of the murder of priests, the rape of nuns, and the destruction of church property. Lurid stories of the crucifixion of nuns and priests and other barbarous acts appeared in the *Pilot.*[39] In the fall of 1936, the *Pilot* authoritatively concluded that the Spanish Civil War had evolved from a confrontation between Reds and fascists to "a fight to the finish between the defenders of religion, order, and decency and their opponents."[40] Cardinal O'Connell fully concurred. His eminence described General Franco "as a fighter for Christian civilization in Spain" after Franco's planes killed a thousand civilians in Barcelona on March 18, 1938.[41]

The Spanish Civil War became such a crucial issue because it appeared to be "so clear-cut." American liberals perceived it to be a case of democracy confronting fascism. Irish Catholics believed it to be a clear battle between "Christianity and civilization with Communism and barbarism." The ethnic differences were unmistakable. "Almost to a man the hierarchy and the American Catholic press supported the Franco side, insisting that the loyalist government was communist dominated, did not represent the will of the Spanish people, and was bent upon the destruction of the Church in Spain." The explicit support that prominent New Dealers gave to the loyalist government alienated Irish Catholics, heightening a defensiveness and "minority consciousness" that flowered in the late 1930s and early

1940s.[42] The international arena, therefore, played a crucial role in straining interethnic relations.

In Boston, Irish opposition to communism and hence support for the European authoritarian and fascist governments in Spain, Portugal, and Austria exacerbated further the already strained relationships between Boston's Irish and Jewish communities. In this atmosphere of increasing ethnic tensions, Irish Catholics felt compelled to assert an excessively strident ethnic identity. This was clearly the case when the *Pilot* discussed the "fundamental" differences between communist and fascist subversion:

> The fact is that "Fascism," wherever it is, is not susceptible to export. It is a product peculiar to the nation of its origin. It emphasizes national beginnings, rediscovers the source of national pride. If Fascism is bad, it will affect exclusively a local people, a national group. Fascism is not a universal culture.
>
> But Communism is all things Fascism is not. Communism is a universal ideology. It minimizes nation and race; it reduces to nothing merely local considerations in favor of a world aspiration.
>
> If both sides are practicing subversive activities, the Communist is the more dangerous agent. Besides our money and our moral support, he wants ourselves. He hopes for a Sovietized America.[43]

The distinctions made by the *Pilot* went right to the heart of a Boston Irish Catholic outlook. In vigorously endorsing anticommunism, Boston's Irish community "could demonstrate the compatibility of their faith and patriotism" with traditional American values.[44] In closing its eyes to the inherent dangers of fascism, the *Pilot* embraced another solidly American tradition—isolationism. Thus excessive preoccupation with anticommunism and isolationism led Boston's influential Irish church to dismiss a number of fundamental issues involved in the European conflagration. With an insensitivity born of ethnic frustrations and bitterness, the *Pilot* pointed out that no European power could be found guiltless of Hitlerism. The *Pilot* concluded that Britain and the Soviet Union were just as callous as Germany. Unlike Germany, however, Britain and the Soviet Union were "expert at making black appear white."[45] The editors of the *Pilot*, like Father Coughlin, accepted the revisionist thesis that British propaganda, organized industrial greed, and pro-British support accounted for American participation in World War I. The *Pilot* concluded that these same forces were at work in 1939. Indeed, throughout the 1930s, Boston's Irish Catholics railed against the real and imagined biases of non-Irish America. The Boston Irish complained that Catholic persecution in Mexico, the pillaging of the church in Spain, and even historic Irish oppression at British hands were not accorded the recognition or the sympathy given the persecution of the Jews in Germany by liberal America.[46] Although neither Cardinal O'Connell nor the editors of the *Pilot* were anti-Semitic, the similarities between a Boston Irish Catholic outlook and Father Coughlin's shrill defensiveness were nonetheless apparent. The *Pilot*, like Father Coughlin's *Social Justice*, saw in international communism a direct and tangible menace at the root of the most threatening international crisis of the 1930s. Like *Social Justice*, the *Pilot* translated these perceptions into vigorous support for the excessive Red-baiting of the Dies Committee.[47]

Cardinal O'Connell and the editors of the *Pilot* were not the only members of the Boston Irish community preoccupied with the international system. The community's two most influential organizations, the Knights of Columbus and the Catholic Order of Foresters, loudly denounced the excesses of communism in Mexico, Spain, and the Soviet Union. In addition, the Knights of Columbus and the Catholic Order of Foresters raised their voices in opposition to American involvement in European affairs.[48] Similarly, international issues and events preoccupied Irish Catholic students at Boston College. The political and social upheaval of the 1930s tended to heighten the salience of ethnic identity among Boston College men as it did in the church and in the neighborhoods of Boston.[49]

Like Boston's Irish community as a whole, Boston College students shared an outlook they expressed in isolationism, anticommunism, and a shrill defensiveness.[50] An editorial in the *Boston College Heights* illustrated this outlook. Deploring the barbarous treatment of Protestants, Catholics, and Jews in Germany, the editors concluded:

> The first-page treatment of the current affronteries calls to mind with far too great ease the few last page paragraphs devoted to the outrages in Mexico and Spain.

Agreement may be had with the protests of Nazi butchery, but can anyone blame us for experiencing profound sorrow at the graphic pictures of ruined churches in Mexico and Spain, of slaughtered nuns and martyred priests?

The reticence, the half-told tales in the secular press demonstrate a most self-conscious neutrality on the question of Catholic persecution . . . . let us not forget the tens of thousands of Catholics who were murdered in Spain.[51]

These views were appalling to many members of Boston's Jewish community. In particular, the *Jewish Advocate* delivered a stinging rebuke to the *Pilot* for repeatedly complaining that several major American newspapers published Nazi attacks against activities of the Catholic church in Germany without any refutation. The *Advocate* stated: "the same applies equally well to Catholic papers and to Catholic speakers whose voice is heard by millions over the air. We hope that the *Pilot* will apply its complaints equally well to the sinners among members of its own faith."[52] Although the church's role was hardly anti-Semitic, its defensiveness did contribute to the rising tensions that Father Coughlin exploited in Boston as the *Advocate* implied. Certainly Boston's influential Catholic church and its related institutions contributed to the polarization of the Hub's ethnic enclaves. But the impact of the international system on the exacerbation of ethnic conflict was manifest in Boston's political community as well.

THE POLITICIZATION OF ETHNICITY: IRISH POLITICS, ETHNIC CONFLICT, AND THE INTERNATIONAL SYSTEM

The career of Massachusetts' senior senator, David I. Walsh, illustrated the import of the international environment as well as the salience of enthnicity in Massachusetts politics. Senator Walsh began his career as a vigorous supporter of Woodrow Wilson's international aspirations. However, the hostility generated by Wilson's unfulfilled pledge of self-determination for suppressed European nationalities overwhelmingly alienated Walsh's primary constituency—the Irish of Massachusetts, the mainstays of the Bay State's Democratic party.[53] Walsh realized the importance of the international environment, particularly its relationship to ethnicity, and was careful not to offend the state's Irish in the future. Without large pluralities in the Bay State's industrial ethnic strongholds— Boston, Brockton, Fall River, Lawrence, Lowell, and New Bedford—Yankee Republican strength in rural Massachusetts would have swept Walsh out of office. Thus David I. Walsh, like his counterparts in Boston's Catholic hierarchy, shrilly articulated a defensive and shortsighted isolationism. "Which are the enemies of democracy and which are the democracies seeking to thwart them," Senator Walsh asked the Senate on April 17, 1939. "Are we as a government ready to set ourselves up as a judge between the simon-pure democracy assumed by some nations which are and have been for centuries notorious imperialists and other nations obsessed by grandiose complexes and devoted to authoritarian theories and totalitarian systems," he demanded.

> Is it any legitimate concern of ours for purposes of friendly commercial intercourse, or for any other purpose, what form of government a foreign people embrace or how they happen to embrace it, unless, of course, it should be fundamentally obnoxious to standards of morals, decency, and justice that ordinarily have obtained in the past between civilized peoples and which would disturb our own security?
>
> It is utterly unthinkable that we should at this time, or any other time, or for any reason except our own self-protection, join with any foreign group or block of nations in a pledge or understanding designed to check by moral coercion or implication of physical force the proposed action of any other nation.[54]

Senator Walsh's isolationism received the emphatic approval of Boston's Irish community.[55] It is hardly surprising that David I. Walsh was one of the Senate's staunchest proponents of American neutrality. Boston's Irish dissatisfaction with the foreign and domestic policies of the New Deal extended to all governmental levels, however.

Irish members of the Boston City Council and the school committee were preoccupied by the international scene. These grassroots politicians reflected the currents of opinion in Boston's Irish neighborhoods no less accurately than Massachusetts' influential congressional delegation. City councilors, school committeemen, state legislators, and union officials were in touch with the residents of Boston's Irish enclaves on a day-to-day basis. The city council frequently considered the impact of international developments in Boston. The city council possessed the ability to initiate the legislative process in the form of requests for information from the mayor. This technique enabled members of the city council to express their views of foreign and domestic issues normally outside of their traditional purview.[56]

Thus the supposed excesses of communist organizations preoccupied many of the Irish members of the city council. Red-baiting evolved into one of the council's favorite pastimes. Repeatedly, its Irish members passed orders vigorously supporting the work of the Dies Committee and calling for its help in rooting out subversives in Boston.[57] Similarly, Irish members of the Massachusetts General Court were fascinated by the specter of communist advances in Europe as well as in the Bay State. In 1935 the general court established a Teacher's Loyalty Oath with the vigorous support of Irish members of the state house. In 1937-38 State Senator Thomas Dorgan of South Boston and other Irish politicians launched their own local Red Scare. The state legislature originally established a special commission to investigate the activities of communist organizations within the commonwealth. But the outcry of Boston's Jewish community forced these ever vigilant legislators to include within their definition of subversives fascists and Nazi organizations as well.[58] Frequently, the commission conducted hearings in comic opera fashion. For example, the commission asked witnesses "whether they knew the meaning of Boogwuzzies (bourgeoisie) or whether they planned to liquefy the Church."[59] An Irish member of the city council characterized Harvard as "a hotbed of radicalism" noting "I want to ask what they expect of a university that teaches its football players how to dance."[60]

On a somewhat more serious note, the commission grilled a Jewish graduate student at Harvard, Morrison Sharp, who had run for Congress on the People's Labor Ticket in the 1936 election. State Senator Thomas M. Burke of Dorchester, convinced of the subversive character of Mr. Sharp's activities, tried to ascertain how

many members of Harvard's faculty were involved. In a similar
fashion, when Philip Frankfeld, secretary of the Massachusetts
Communist party, refused to produce the names of twelve hundred
Massachusetts residents who were members of the Communist
party, Senator Burke tried another tact to prove his point. "Do you
believe in God," Burke demanded.[61] Such obvious Red-baiting and
blatant bigotry outraged Boston's conservative Republican newspaper, the Boston Traveler. The Traveler deplored such mudsling-
ing. "Frankfeld's answer should have been that it was none of
Burke's business, nor the state's business whether he believed in
God, that is a matter between himself and his conscience." The
Traveler argued: "In Russia, a person suffers deprivations of certain rights if he believes in God. We trust Senator Burke hasn't it in
mind to impose penalties here on persons who do not believe in
God. In this hearing, God can get along perfectly well without
Senator Burke's political help."[62]

Not unexpectedly, the commission found little evidence of fascist
inroads in Boston despite the support accorded Father Coughlin's
Christian Front in South Boston and Dorchester. The commission
did concede that Boston's Italian newspapers were "sympathetic to
Fascism in Italy." In addition, the report stated that some Italian
groups were "still loyal to the tradition of their homeland." On the
whole, the commission attempted to reassure the commonwealth
that, "There is no evidence, however, that they are engaged in any
effort to carry the doctrines of Fascism into effect in this land of
their adoption." Undoubtedly, it was the specter of communist activities in the Bay State that presented the greatest threat to the
citizens of Massachusetts. As the commission concluded: ". . . in-
dications point more to an imposition of totalitarianism from the
left rather than the right. The Commission is of the belief that the
present widespread alarm concerning Fascism in America is, in
large part, the result of artful propaganda planned and inspired by
the Communist Party and widely spread by its satellites and allies."[63]

Perhaps the most significant instances of ethnic conflict from a
political perspective, based on the impact of the international environment, occurred in the Boston School Committee. Like the city
council and the state legislature, Irish preoccupation with anticom-

munism defined the specific issue. Its larger implications went a long way to explaining the dynamics of rising ethnic tensions in Boston.[64]

In 1939 a group of Jewish students at Roxbury Memorial High School organized a discussion group under the auspices of the American Student Union. Their goal was to discuss all sides of contemporary international politics such as the Spanish Civil War, American neutrality, and the rise of fascism in Europe. After only two meetings of the discussion group in which the American Neutrality Act and the Spanish Embargo were discussed, Robert Masterson, headmaster of Roxbury High, publicly denounced these students before a senior assembly.[65] Headmaster Masterson charged that the students were "entering into alliances against the government," creating "insulting...street demonstrations" and attacking "a largely attended church in Boston." In addition, Masterson and several teachers under his direction threatened the students, all high school seniors, with dismissal from school without their diplomas. Masterson claimed to be upholding his moral and professional duty to safeguard the school's remaining students from "subversive" and "communistic" activities.[66] The American Student Union was at the time a communist-front organization. The interactions between the international arena and ethnic conflict in Boston were dramatically illustrated in the ensuing battle.

The only non-Irish member of the Boston School Committee, Joseph Lee, brought the conflict to a head. Lee, a member of one of Boston's wealthiest Brahmin families and one of the few Brahmins actively to engage in Boston politics, bristled with indignation. Outraged by what he saw as blatant misuse of power in a democratic society, Lee denounced the coercive methods used by Masterson and his staff to stifle discussion of the Spanish Civil War. "Untold and fearful harm has been done already by the school systems' hostile attitude toward those who would remain even openminded toward the Spanish Republic," Lee asserted.[67] For Joseph Lee, such acts of bigotry and intolerance demonstrated the direct intrusion of the international system in Boston. Thus Lee warned the other members of the school committee and his fellow Bostonians:

By being local party to a campaign of pressure tactics brought to kill the Administration's policy which favored lifting the embargo on Spain in the interest of the Spanish government, they have helped to bring the Rome-Berlin axis a thousand miles nearer to America; have aided in bottling up the Mediterranean against England and in favor of the Dictators, and have given the Dictators a jumping off place to South America, which they have been cultivating much more successfully than the United States. I say to this School Committee and to the public of Boston that boys now in school will lie dead on battlefields, as a result of those whose thoughtless and intemperate foreign and domestic policies are manifest in the un-American intimidation which they have so far condoned at Roxbury Memorial High School.[68]

The Irish members of the school committee saw the incident in a rather different light. For Henry J. Smith, Chairman, Dr. Patrick J. Foley, Frederick R. Sullivan, and Joseph C. White the problem was clear-cut—the threat of communist subversion in the schools of Boston. From the outset, the central issue for the Irish majority was that the American Student Union was indeed a subversive organization.[69] City Councilor William J. Galvin of South Boston charged that the American Student Union resulted from "a united front gathering of young Socialists and Communists."[70] Moreover, Galvin reported to the city council that the American Student Union ". . . was formerly known as the Student League of Industrial Democracy and the National Student League. The latter was the American section of the Proletarian Youth League of Moscow."[71] Frederick R. Sullivan, a member of both the Boston School Committee and the Boston City Council, fully concurred with Galvin. He was even more outspoken in his analysis of the problems facing the school committee and the city of Boston. Calling Lee a communist, Sullivan demanded his impeachment. "I believe if the statement is not denied that Mr. Lee is definitely a Communist, actively so, having been affiliated with communistic organizations, that if that body has jurisdiction over its membership it should impeach the fifth member of the Boston School Committee." Speaking of Lee and other liberals, Sullivan asserted: "Needless to say, it is to the Red Government at Barcelona that they wish the arms shipped. They are moved by the desperate straits in which the government finds itself at present." Yet ethnic animosities were never very far from the surface during the length of the crisis. Sullivan concluded: "I am amazed, under the circumstances, to find Mr. Lee speaking of the brotherhood of man and his love for his fellow citizens. Only a few years ago he came out with one of the most vile statements against the descendants of the Irish race in South Boston. This is the man who has such an outstanding love of and so ardent devotion to the brotherhood of man."[72]

The Irish members of the Boston School Committee apparently saw nothing coercive or arbitrary about Headmaster Masterson's action. For they immediately provided Masterson with a vote of confidence and shortly thereafter sent him a personal letter of commendation. Joseph Lee was the lone dissenter in each case.[73]

But the issue refused to die. For over a year this acrimonious debate dragged on.[74] The influential journal *School and Society* sardonically noted: "The high-minded methods of the School Committee and its failure to consider the problem of free speech which lies at the heart of all such controversies must be disillusioning to the children whom it claims to be protecting from un-American influences."[75]

Like *School and Society*, Joseph Lee pointed to the larger questions involved in this conflict. First and foremost, Lee recognized the fundamental ethnic issues at stake. Citing Irish Catholicism as the single most important influence in the life of Boston's public school system, Lee pleaded for more tolerance and objectivity in the framing of school policies. Lee suggested that the fundamental challenges facing the government and the citizens of Boston during a period of international turmoil were the successful implementation of policies based on freedom and tolerance.[76] Lee argued that such a tolerant perspective was compromised by an excessively strident ethnic outlook particularly when the political stands of the Catholic church came into play. "If the Catholic Church is a bulwark against Communism, why do people identified with that faith keep pointing to organizations that have no connection whatever with Communism and call them Communistic," Lee asked. He argued that it was not the religion of the church that created tensions and anxieties for Boston's non-Catholics, but those political issues that the church embraced.[77] Consequently, issues such as isolationism, fascism, and communism became infused with highly explosive ethnic overtones. "It just seems that the majority of the School Committee are able to exercise absolute tolerance in all personal and religious relations," Lee concluded, "and yet when you get out into questions of our own international relations, without having a free discussion of the points of view, a person is branded as alien to the government or as a subversive, if the stand of that person does not square with the stand that the Church has taken on those matters."[78]

In this atmosphere, political, religious, and cultural institutions contributed to rising ethnic tensions in Boston in the latter years of the 1930s. No single factor determined the precise nature of Irish hostility toward Yankees, Jews, and liberals. Rather a number of factors converged. Certainly the role played by Father Charles E. Coughlin was a significant one at least for the Irish of South Boston. The radio priest received the bulk of his support from the working-class Irish neighborhoods of South Boston, Charlestown, and Dorchester. He effectively fused domestic dissatisfaction to international insecurities. In so doing, Coughlin helped to legitimate anti-Semitism in South Boston and Charlestown when the socioeconomic disorientations of the depression years were still acute. However, Father Coughlin's influence was uneven at best in Boston's Irish neighborhoods.

Unquestionably, a hardcore of maladjusted and discontented men and women supported his ideas and organizations after 1937. But this explicit reliance on anti-Semitism was not a respectable prejudice for the majority of Boston's political and religious leaders in the 1930s and 1940s. Here again international issues and events helped to shape the specific dimensions of ethnic conflict in Boston. Anti-Semitic overtones often very subtly crept into the anticommunist and isolationist rhetoric of the Boston Irish. On face value alone both anticommunism and isolationism were respectable causes in contrast to anti-Semitism during the 1930s. Moreover, in anticommunism and isolationism the Boston Irish reaffirmed a solidly American ideological outlook—an identity wholly compatible with traditional American ideals and values. Further, in their opposition to communism the Boston Irish demonstrated, at least in theory, a commitment to the values of freedom and democracy.

Anticommunism, in other words, was a way of proving the Americanism of their ethnic inheritance—Irish Catholicism. Similarly, the Boston Irish demonstrated the compatibility of their Irish ethnicity and American citizenship by embracing isolationism. Isolationism also gave respectability to their still acute Anglophobia.

However, anticommunism and isolationism contributed to ethnic conflict in Boston because they tended to house community-wide frustrations and resentments. Anticommunism and isolationism became respectable reasons for resenting Jewish insensitivities or Yankee prejudices. Although Boston's most respectable religious and political leaders were hardly anti-Semitic, the lack of effective political and ecclesiastical leadership created a void in which a minority consciousness flourished. Indeed, the historic defensiveness and rancor of the Boston Irish further diminished ideological or analytical clarity among anti-Semitic, anticommunist, and isolationist rhetoric. In a kind of collective whine, the Boston Irish too often embraced a ghettoized view of themselves and outsiders that the impact of international events only heightened. The "we-they" dichotomy surfaced in the specter of communism in Mexico and Spain. Thus American Catholics perceived a situation in which liberals, Yankees, and Jews were arrayed against persecuted and despised Catholics. Whereas this perspective was noticeable in the American Catholic community as a whole—it was absolutely pronounced in Irish Boston. The psychological weight of Boston's past, socioeconomic failures, and conservative political and religious elites fostered this defensiveness throughout the 1930s in the Hub's Irish sections.

The very nature of Boston's Irish political, religious, and cultural institutions tended to mute direct ethnic conflict. Unlike the catharsis that the Italo-Ethiopian War constituted in the Italian North End and East Boston, Irish defensiveness and rancor were less explicit. As in any ghetto, the victims often internalize the most debilitating dimensions of the culture. In the close-knit and insular environment of South Boston, ethnic conflict was found in overt anti-Semitic acts as well as through innuendo. An Irish subculture channeled ethnic hostilities through a number of code words—liberal, atheistic, pink, subversive, communist. These often subtle distinctions summoned forth Irish contempt, bitterness, and frustrations with non-Irish values and ideals. Although repeated instances of direct and hostile ethnic conflict were somewhat rare, the impact of these half-articulated hostilities was nonetheless real. They contributed to a profound psychological and cultural uneasiness ultimately permeating the institutional structure of Irish Boston. This sustained uneasiness contributed to the further polarizing of Boston's ethnic enclaves.

During these difficult and troubled years, Boston's Italians and Jews, no less than the Irish, struggled to reconcile the deteriorating international environment with life in Boston. Like the Boston Irish, the Hub's Italians and Jews sought to define themselves and their places in American life amid a chaotic and unstable international system.

NOTES

1. Charles J. Tull, *Father Coughlin and the New Deal* (Syracuse, N.Y.: Syracuse University Press, 1965), p. 22.

2. William V. Shannon, *The American Irish* (New York: Macmillan Co., 1963), p. 304.

3. Ibid., pp. 296, 303; David J. O'Brien, *American Catholics and Social Reform, The New Deal Years* (New York: Oxford University Press, 1968), pp. 161-69; Sheldon Marcus, *Father Coughlin, The Tumultuous Life of the Priest of the Little Flower* (Boston: Little, Brown & Co., 1973), p. 37; Tull, *Father Coughlin and the New Deal*, pp. 51-58.

4. Rev. Charles E. Coughlin, *Eight Lectures on Labor, Capital and Justice* (Royal Oak, Mich.: Radio League of the Little Flower, 1934), pp. 35-40, 42-45; Rev. Charles E. Coughlin, *Series of Lectures on Social Justice March 1935* (Royal Oak, Mich.: The Radio League of the Little Flower, 1935), pp. 12, 76-78, 80-83, 112-17, 125-26, 132-34; O'Brien, *American Catholics and Social Reform*, pp. 161, 162-69.

5. Shannon, *The American Irish*, p. 308; Marcus, *Father Coughlin*, p. 83; Selig Adler, *The Isolationist Impulse, Its Twentieth-Century Reaction* (London: Abelard-Schuman, 1957), pp. 254-55; Robert A. Devine, *The Illusion of Neutrality, Franklin D. Roosevelt and the Struggle Over the Arms Embargo* (Chicago: Quadrangle Press, 1962) pp. 83-84.

6. Shannon, *The American Irish*, p. 310.

7. See, for example, Rev. Charles E. Coughlin, *16 Radio Lectures, 1938 Series* (Detroit: Condon Printing Co., 1938), pp. 4-11, 40-46; Rev. Charles E. Coughlin, *Why Leave Our Own? 13 Addresses on Christianity and*

Americanism January 8-April 2, 1939 (Detroit: The Inland Press, 1939), pp. 4-162; *Social Justice,* 3 April 1936; 24 April 1936; 15 May 1936; 6 July 1936; 3 August 1936; 10 August 1936; 17 August 1936; 5 October 1936; 26 October 1936; 23 November 1936; 30 November 1936; 21 June 1937; 30 August 1937; 17 January 1938; 21 March 1938; 16 May 1938; 18 July 1938; 25 July 1938; 1 August 1936; 26 November 1938; 2 January 1939; 16 January 1939; 23 January 1939; 27 February 1939; 1 May 1939; 5 June 1939; 18 September 1939; 2 October 1939; 13 November 1939; Shannon, *The American Irish,* p. 315.

8. For representative statements, see *Social Justice,* 21 February 1938.

9. *The Protocols of the Elders of Zion* first appeared in the July 18, 1938, issue of *Social Justice* and was carried in installments throughout the fall and winter of 1938-39.

10. Coughlin's opposition to the entrance of European immigrants illustrated his growing preoccupation with the international system. "America has been called the melting pot. Nevertheless, it is impossible to melt the dross of atheism, the scavengery of Communism, and the offal of internationalism with any success into the substance of sound Americanism . . . . let our government recognize the necessity of sterilizing the minds and fumigating the souls of every immigrant who seeks refuge behind the Statue of Liberty." *Social-Justice,* 16 May 1938.

11. The weekly editions of *Social Justice* document these trends between 1937 and 1941.

12. Tull, *Father Coughlin and the New Deal,* pp. 86, 141.

13. Coughlin justified the persecution of the Jews in Germany as a defense mechanism against communism during a broadcast delivered on Sunday, November 20, 1938; Coughlin, *Why Leave Our Own?,* pp. 43-59; *Social Justice,* 1 August 1936; 25 July 1938; 20 November 1938; 2 January 1939. *Social Justice* reveals the full force of Coughlin's anti-Semitism: 29 June 1936; 12 October 1936; 30 November 1936; 7 December 1936; 11 October 1936; 8 March 1937; 1 February 1938; 16 May 1938; 25 July 1938; 1 August 1938; 2 January 1939; 16 January 1939; 30 January 1939; 6 February 1939; 7 February 1939; 13 February 1939; 20 February 1939; 12 June 1939; 19 June 1939; 24 June 1939. See also Tull, *Father Coughlin and the New Deal,* pp. 86, 141.

14. Tull, *Father Coughlin and the New Deal,* pp. 189-91; Marcus, *Father Coughlin,* p. 192; Coughlin, *16 Radio Lectures, 1938 Series,* pp. 96-99; Ronald H. Bayor, *Neighbors in Conflict, The Irish, Germans, Jews and Italians of New York City, 1929-1941* (Baltimore: Johns Hopkins University Press, 1978) pp. 97-103.

15. James Michael Curley, *I'd Do It Again* (Englewood Cliffs, N.J.: Prentice Hall, 1957), pp. 296-98; Tull, *Father Coughlin and the New Deal,*

p. 101; Charles H. Trout, "Boston During the Great Depression 1928-1940" (Ph.D diss., Columbia University, 1972), p. 592.

16. Trout, "Boston During the Great Depression," p. 341; Tull, *Father Coughlin and the New Deal*, p. 101.

17. One major political leader actively engaged in Boston politics during the 1930s, who wanted to remain anonymous, suggested to the author that contemporary Boston politicos believed that 90 percent of South Boston's Irish supported Father Coughlin. The figure is probably an exaggeration but it does illustrate the extent to which contemporaries feared Coughlin's strength in South Boston. In the final analysis, however, the Boston Irish overwhelmingly chose Franklin D. Roosevelt.

18. The congressmen were: Joseph Casey, 3rd Congressional District; Arthur Healey, 8th Congressional District; and John Higgins, 11th Congressional District.

19. J. F. Welch to O'Connell, 9 December 1934; Unsigned letter to O'Connell, 18 December 1934; William Henry O'Connell Papers, Archives of the Archdiocese of Boston, Brighton, Massachusetts.

20. James Meaney to O'Connell, 18 April 1932; William Henry O'Connell Papers. Mr. Meaney continued: "Father Coughlin is a man who has tried to show the common working people the way they are being neglected by those in power; how they are the last to be considered in the way of taxes. He is a noble man and has millions of friends who make it a point never to miss his radio talks; no matter where they are, arrangement is made to be somewhere that there is a radio at 4 P.M. Sundays to hear Father Coughlin. His name is a household word....He is in my opinion a God-sent man to try to help the poor...."

21. O'Brien, *American Catholics and Social Reform*, p. 175.

22. Lawrence Fuchs, *Political Behavior of American Jews* (Glencoe, Ill.: The Free Press, 1956), p. 138, points out that the core of Coughlin's support in Boston came from "...Irish strongholds where anti-Semitism flourished." Similarly, Samuel Lubell's study of the 1936 election concluded that "something like ten to fifteen percent of Boston's Jewish and Catholic vote fluctuated in mutual hostility." See Lubell, *The Future of American Politics*, 3d ed. (New York: Harper & Row, 1963), p. 213; Tull, *Father Coughlin and the New Deal*, p. 170; Trout, "Boston During the Great Depression," pp. 595, 604.

23. Boston, Mass: *Report of the Election Department of the City of Boston*, 1936, no. 11, p. 70; Curley, *I'd Do It Again*, p. 298.

24. O'Brien, *American Catholics and Social Reform*, p. 175; Shannon, *The American Irish*, p. 315; Bayor, *Neighbors in Conflict*, pp. 155-62; *Jewish Advocate*, 30 June 1936; Wallace Stegner, "The Radio Priest and His

Flock," in *The Aspirin Age 1919-1941*, ed. Isabel Leighton, (New York: Simon & Schuster, 1949), pp. 250-52.

25. *Social Justice*, 14 August 1939; for similar stories dealing with Irish-Jewish relations in New York City, see 16 January 1939; 20 February 1939.

26. Lawrence J. McCaffrey, *The Irish Diaspora in America* (Bloomington: Indiana University Press, 1976), pp. 78-79.

27. Trout, "Boston During the Great Depression," p. 530.

28. X to O'Connell, 10 July 1920; William Henry O'Connell Papers. O'Connell's papers reveal an extensive collection of letters from religious and lay Catholics all over the world between 1907 and 1944. Information about contemporary issues and events was invariably exchanged. In particular, O'Connell received many eye-witness accounts of the Spanish Civil War and the persecution of the church in Mexico.

29. Tull, *Father Coughlin and the New Deal*, pp. 19, 77, 98.

30. *Boston Pilot*, 28 March 1936.

31. Ibid., 25 March 1935; 27 April 1935; 15 February 1936; 8 May 1937; 10 July 1937; 26 November 1938; 28 October 1938; 4 January 1939.

32. Historian David O'Brien has perceptively assessed the importance of the international system of the 1930s and an Irish Catholic sense of ethnic identity: "The recognition of Russia, the apathy toward religious persecution in Mexico, and most importantly, the near unanimous opposition of articulate American opinion to the Catholic position on the Spanish Civil War, all worked to perpetuate among American Catholics the sense of alienation and minority consciousness which had dominated their thought since the middle of the nineteenth century." *American Catholics and Social Reform*, p. 67.

33. Trout, "Boston During the Great Depression," p. 591.

34. Ibid., p. 531.

35. *Boston Pilot*, 25 January 1935; 25 March 1935; 27 March 1935; 10 July 1937.

36. "Americans generally were apathetic, but prominent liberals publicly deprecated reports of persecution because of the Church's ties with the aristocracy and counterrevolutionary classes. . . . In particular, they [American Catholics] could not understand the failure of people who normally championed religious liberty to demonstrate some concern for its violation in a neighboring country. They were bound to see this situation as another expression of the bigotry they experienced in 1928, a manifestation of their own second class citizenship." O'Brien, *American Catholics and Social Reform*, p. 80.

37. *Boston Pilot*, 23 February 1935; 28 December 1935.

38. Ibid., 1 June 1935.

39. Ibid., 11 July 1935; 8 August 1935; 29 August 1935; 5 September 1936; 3 October 1936; 30 January 1937; 19 February 1938; 25 June 1938.

40. Ibid., 3 October 1936.

41. Trout, "Boston During the Great Depression," p. 532.

42. O'Brien, *American Catholics and Social Reform*, pp. 86, 89.

43. *Boston Pilot*, 27 May 1937.

44. O'Brien, *American Catholics and Social Reform*, p. 96.

45. *Boston Pilot*, 16 September 1939.

46. Ibid., 25 March 1939; 6 May 1939; 25 August 1939.

47. Ibid., 3 September 1938; 15 April 1939; 3 June 1939.

48. Ibid., 12 January 1935; 29 January 1935; 24 August 1935; *Boston College Heights*, 17 October 1934; 5 December 1934; Knights of Columbus Papers and Catholic Order of Foresters Papers, Archives of the Archdiocese of Boston, Brighton, Massachusetts.

49. An editorial in the *Boston College Heights* lauded the establishment of a Department of Gaelic Language and Literature at Boston College in September 1939. The *Heights* called for a greater recognition of the Irish contribution to the college. "Boston College has been predominantly Irish in its faculty and student body since its foundation. Yet in all the years that have passed since then, the culture and speech of the race of most of its sons have been neglected." *Boston College Heights*, 29 September 1939.

50. Ibid., 17 October 1934; 20 October 1934; 5 December 1934; 12 December 1934; 5 February 1935; 10 April 1935; 13 January 1939; 19 January 1939; 29 September 1939.

51. Ibid., 9 December 1938.

52. *Jewish Advocate*, 2 July 1939.

53. J. Joseph Huthmacher, *Massachusetts People and Politics 1919-1933* (Cambridge: Harvard University Press, 1959), pp. 22-26.

54. David I. Walsh, "Keep America Out of War," *Vital Speeches*, 5 (May 15, 1939): 451-52.

55. See chapter 5 for an analysis of Senator Walsh's isolationism in the 1940s.

56. Trout, "Boston During the Great Depression," p. 74.

57. Boston, Mass., *Report of the Proceedings of the City Council of the City of Boston*, March 29, 1937, p. 120; June 28, 1937, p. 324; January 9, 1939, p. 15; February 14, 1939, pp. 74-75; September 8, 1939, p. 42; (hereafter cited as *City Council Proceedings*).

58. Commonwealth of Massachusetts, *Journal of the Massachusetts House*, April 21, 1937, p. 869; Trout, "Boston During the Great Depression," p. 528.

59. Trout, "Boston During the Great Depression," p. 259, as quoted in

Robert M. Lovett, "Witch-Hunting in Massachusetts," *New Republic*, 1 December 1937, pp. 96-97; "Red Purge, Boston Style," ibid., 22 June 1938, p. 173.

60. *City Council Proceedings*, May 6, 1940, p. 202.

61. Commonwealth of Massachusetts Transcript of the *Special Commission to Investigate the Activities Within the Commonwealth of Communistic, Fascist, Nazi and Other Subversive Organizations, 1937* [Hearings at Gardner Auditorium, State House, Boston, Massachusetts], Monday, November 15, 1937, p. 140, Massachusetts State Archives, Boston, Massachusetts.

62. Ibid., p. 13.

63. Ibid., pp. 12, 13.

64. Boston, Mass., *Report of the Proceedings of the School Committee of the City of Boston*, February 6, 1939, pp. 9, 24-27, (hereafter cited as *School Committee Proceedings*).

65. Ibid., February 6, 1939, p. 24; February 13, 1939, pp. 34-37.

66. Ibid., February 6, 1939, pp. 26-27; February 13, 1939, pp. 35-36.

67. Ibid., February 13, 1939, p. 35.

68. Ibid.

69. Ibid., February 6, 1939, p. 25; February 13, 1939, p. 36; September 8, 1939, pp. 173-78.

70. *City Council Proceedings*, February 14, 1939, p. 82.

71. Ibid.

72. Ibid., pp. 82, 83. Sullivan alluded to a statement made by Lee during his tenure on the Boston Housing Committee, which had recommended an area in South Boston as the site for a Works Project Administration housing project that "merely low-grade Irish, Poles, and Lithuanians" would be displaced. He was roundly denounced by Boston's Irish politicians at the time. See Trout, "Boston During the Great Depression," p. 556.

73. *School Committee Proceedings*, February 6, 1939, p. 26; February 13, 1939, pp. 36-37.

74. Ibid., September 18, 1939, pp. 172-78; December 4, 1939, p. 229; July 22, 1940, p. 128.

75. "Civil Liberties in the Schools," *School and Society* 44 (March 11, 1935):319-20.

76. *School Committee Proceedings*, June 26, 1939, pp. 136-37.

77. Ibid., pp. 138, 139.

78. Ibid., pp. 139-40.

4

Ethnic Conflict in Boston: Italian and Jewish Perspectives, 1935-1939

Legacies of past injustices and the "weight" of Boston's history helped to set the stage for rising ethnic tensions that would envelop the city in the 1940s. But it was the impact of international issues and events that defined the scope and intensity of ethnic conflict in Boston. Boston's Italians and Jews responded to many of the most important international issues and events of the 1930s: the Italo-Ethiopian War, the Spanish Civil War, German aggression, anticommunism, isolationism, neutrality, Zionism, and anti-Semitism.

MUSSOLINI AND BOSTON'S ITALIANS: THE QUEST FOR ETHNIC SELF-IDENTITY

"Italy is, in some ways, a concept as much as a country," historian John Diggins pointed out: "For nineteenth century Americans, it was a state of mind as well as a nation-state. Somewhere between the idea and the reality hovered a geographical abstraction that beguiled the imagination."[1] Well into the 1930s, Italy continued to cast a powerful shadow over the American landscape. Italy's charismatic leader, Benito Mussolini, occupied a central position in the American view of Italy. Throughout the 1920s and up until the brutal Italian invasion of Ethiopia in 1935, Mussolini enjoyed great popularity in the United States. Throughout the 1920s American public opinion differentiated between Mussolini's achievements in Italy and the average first- or second-generation Italian American. The image of the indolent, malevolent, ignorant foreigner lingered.[2] Ironically, one of Mussolini's staunchest supporters, the *Saturday Evening Post*, was one of the most vigorous proponents of immigrant restriction and Aryan supremacy. Italy and Italians presented contradictory images to the America of the twenties and thirties.[3]

Italian American immigrants throughout the United States—in New York, Chicago, San Francisco, and Boston—acutely perceived the contradictions implicit in these American images. The effects of nativism, immigrant restriction, and xenophobia "tormented" many Italian immigrants. The attempt to make Italian immigrants 100 percent American (the Americanization movement) and the immigrant-restriction laws of the 1920s bred frustration, bitterness, and alienation in hundreds of thousands of Italian residents of the United States. The cry "Mannaggia America! (Damn America)" could be heard from Boston's North End to San Francisco's North Beach. In this psychological atmosphere, the triumphs of Benito Mussolini's Italy constituted a tangible symbol of Italian American self-worth and self-esteem.[4] Mussolini's domestic and international triumphs exerted a powerful impact over the mind of Italian Boston. The Italian invasion of Ethiopia in 1936 epitomized the role played by the international system in Boston's Italian community.[5]

On May 11, 1936, over fifty thousand members of Boston's Italian community poured into the streets of East Boston. In a spontaneous demonstration of support for Italian victories in Ethiopia, Boston's Italians chanted "Il Duce, Il Duce, Il Duce" while they hung Haile Selassie in effigy.[6] "The spectacle of an Italian army marching gloriously into Africa and Mussolini's defying the League warmed the hearts of immigrants who were continually told that their country was a second-rate nation and Il Duce a first-rate buffoon."[7] The Italo-Ethiopian War was the first major international event of the 1930s that brought explicit conflicts to the forefront of life in Boston.

Tensions between Italians and Blacks throughout the United States dramatically increased during Italy's Ethiopian campaign.[8]

Boston's Italian American newspapers provided front-page coverage of all dimensions of the war. The press coverage was extensive and sensational justifying Italian aggression in terms ranging from humanitarian concern for the "natives" of Ethiopia to blunt admissions of imperial aspirations.[9] In each case, the press argued that Italy's international "achievements" reflected credibly on the status and self-respect of Italian Americans.[10] An Italian American college student living in Boston's West End during the 1930s succinctly summarized Mussolini's impact on the community: "What ever you . . . may think of Mussolini, you've got to admit one thing. He has done more to get respect for the Italian people than anybody else. The Italians get a lot more respect now than when I started going to school. And you can thank Mussolini for that."[11] In the process of justifying Italian motives in Ethiopia, Boston's Italian press turned against Ethiopian Blacks with savage invective.

Haile Selassie, in particular, became the object of scurrilous attacks. Frequently, these attacks were nothing but blatant and vicious racist diatribes. For example, the influential *Gazzetta del Massachusetts* characterized the Lion of Judah as "stupid and unthinking," "cunning," and "a maudlin barbarian." Moreover, it was asserted that, "If the emperor of Ethiopia really expects the League of Nations to protect him from Mussolini, then he doesn't possess the sense of humor of most of his race." Belittling Haile Selassie's warning that World War II might break out because of Italian aggression in Ethiopia, a columnist for the *Gazzetta del Massachusetts* wrote: "Selassie spoke these prophetic words from beneath a huge umbrella held aloft by one of his slaves, perhaps to ward off the tse-tse flies, which Ethiopians revere along with tree snakes and string-beans. . . . It will be amusing to see him in the triumphant march when Ethiopia is taken and the tribes subjected."[12]

Boston's Italian press did not limit its racist diatribes to Haile Selassie. Lurid stories circulated in the press concerning how Ethiopian slave traders pillaged the jungles of central Africa in search of "black ivory." Further, Boston's profascist Italian American newspapers sought to justify Italian intervention in Ethiopia on humanitarian and Christian principles. The *Gazzetta del Massachusetts* not only denied the Ethiopians a common religious heritage but ultimately rejected their common humanity as well:

Against this type of barbarian, Italy is arrayed today. A cowardly, brutal, merciless type of being, whose favorite pastime is warring on ignorant defenseless blacks, easy to subjugate and carry off into capitivity. If such people, as these Abyssinians, can be termed as Christians, with the faith of God in their hearts, then the mockery of the ages is the lot of all true sons of Christianity. Surely such monstrous deeds have never been bred in Christian company, and to acknowledge the Abyssinians members of the same brotherhood is to profane the sacred memory of the Founder.[13]

Boston's Italian press vigorously exploited the racial dimensions involved in the Italian invasion of Ethiopia. The fierce diatribes hurled against the Ethiopians and all Blacks by extension epitomized heightening ethnic tensions in the Hub. In Boston gang fights and physical attacks never reached the intensity of Italian-Black conflict in New York City. Reports of rampant anti-Italian prejudice in the New York public schools based on Italian victories in Ethiopia were matters of grave concern in Boston, however.[14]

A number of factors lessened ethnic antagonisms in Boston. The city's Black community contained no more than twenty-five thousand members compared with Harlem's enormous enclave. Further, Italian economic penetration did not intrude into Boston's Black South End as it did in Harlem during the 1930s.[15] The geographical isolation of the West End, the North End, and East Boston also helped to avert direct confrontations between Italians and Blacks. But the intensity of anti-Black tensions in Italian Boston demonstrated the reality of ethnic conflict nonetheless. In this respect, the tensions and hostilities that surfaced throughout the United States during the Italo-Ethiopian War represented a collective release of accumulated Italian American frustrations. "The Italian-Americans' behavior during the war sprang from the same wounded sensitivities as their philofascism."[16] Boston's small Black community was a convenient target.

Italian aggression in Ethiopia served as a powerful stimulus for the development of Black ethnic identities throughout the United States. "Black men and brown have indeed been aroused as never before," wrote W.E.B. Du Bois in his 1935 assessment of the Italo-Ethiopian War published in *Foreign Affairs*. "Economic exploitation," Du Bois concluded, "based on the excuse of race prejudice is the program of the white world. Italy states it openly and plainly."[17] Marcus Garvey, the founder of American pan-Africanism, exalted in the strengthening of Black identities, citing the creation of the "new Negro." Garvey argued that the psychological effects of the Ethiopian War heralded a new era of ethnic pride for Blackmen throughout the world.[18]

The ramifications of the Italo-Ethiopian War affected Boston's Black community. William Monroe Trotter, the Hub's foremost Black leader, skillfully channeled the outrage of Boston's Black community into the construction of the Boston Chapter of the National Association for the Advancement of Colored People (NAACP). The effects of Italian aggression in Ethiopia and the rise of Italian racism in Boston tended to heighten the salience of Black identity. Consequently, Boston's NAACP launched a vigorous effort to oppose racial discrimination and prejudice in the city.[19]

A second consequence of Italian-Black ethnic conflict was a categorical rejection of fascism by Boston's Blacks as "a clear and present threat to minority peoples throughout the 1930s."[20] For Boston's Black community, the outbursts of Italian racism confirmed the fundamental contradictions between democracy and fascism. Boston's Black newspaper, the *Guardian*, clearly stated the relationship between fascism and racism. "Figure it out," the *Guardian* asked its readers: "What would happen to colored inhabitants if Fascism succeeded in getting the upper hand in America? In order to develop strength and thrive, Fascism always selects a minority group on which to focus race hatred. Is there any doubt who would be the victims here?"[21] In Boston, conflict between Italians and Blacks heightened the role of racial pride in the South End. Indeed, the Italo-Ethiopian War and the outbreak of ethnic conflict stemming from it in New York, Chicago, and Boston exerted a tremendous impact on Black America.[22]

The Italo-Ethiopian War stirred Boston's Italian community to its depths. Aside from aggravating relations with Boston's Black community, the Hub's Italians launched unprecedented measures to change American foreign policy. In some respects Italian lobbying efforts were first attempts to mobilize the community politically. The success of these measures was stifled by culturally reinforced isolation and anomie. Once again the impact of the international system helped to define Italian American actions.

President Roosevelt's attempt to revise the American Neutrality Laws in the winter of 1935-36 provoked sustained outbursts of Italian hostility in Boston. Roosevelt hoped to secure for his administration further discretionary powers in dealing with belligerent nations. The president sought additional authority to control the export of vital goods such as oil, cotton, and other textile products desperately needed by Italian troops in Ethiopia.[23] In Boston, as in New York, Chicago, and San Francisco, Italian Americans vociferously denounced such action as a betrayal of fundamental American principles. The reaction of Boston's Italian community was significant for it revealed much about the way the city's Italian Americans viewed themselves, their place in America, and their relationships with Italy. In a front-page editorial, the *Gazzetta del Massachusetts* declared:

England and its perfidious League will do their utmost to humble and insult the members of YOUR race, and YOU AS WELL in the very near future.

Already they have turned this Administration pro-British. Your Secretary of State, Cordell Hull, is outspokenly in favor of the British policy. When Congress convenes again next month HE WILL DEMAND that it pass a law giving the President—that is to say, Mr. Hull—a wider scope of power to deal with the Italo-Ethiopian question as he sees fit.

Do YOU know what that MEANS? It means, my poor misguided friend, that Mr. Roosevelt and Mr. Hull will be empowered to clamp the most drastic of all sanctions on American exported goods to Italy—OIL, COTTON, and OTHER VITAL COMMODITIES which as yet have not been officially placed on the "neutrality" gag list. . . .

. . . These same politicians made fools of the members of the Italian race, for not once did they keep a promise, no matter how fervently given. . . .

. . . Tell Congress what you think of their un-American attitude on the Italo-Ethiopian question! Tell Mr. Roosevelt, Mr. Hull, the INTERNATIONAL BANKERS, the puppets of Britain, and their sly brood of radicals and treacherous Communists!

England and the League are TRYING HARD to BREAK Italy's

back. They want America's help to make certain their plan will not fail. THEY MAY GET IT UNLESS YOU ACT AT ONCE![24]

Boston's Italians moved to prevent any American action that would threaten Italian victory in Ethiopia. Mario Renna, one of the North End's most successful businessmen, denounced the Roosevelt administration in a telegram to the Massachusetts congressional delegation for "their unwarranted extensions of action beyond the expressed desire of Congress in the neutrality act."[25] In December 1935, Italians from all over New England formed the League of American Neutrality claiming a constituency of all ethnic, racial, and religious groups. The league lobbied effectively in New England exerting considerable pressure on the entire New England congressional delegation.[26] Congressman John Higgins, whose district included the North End and East Boston, succumbed to the pressure exerted by Boston's Italian community when he concluded that F.D.R.'s neutrality stance was sponsored by the Carnegie Endowment for Peace—an obvious tool of the League of Nations.[27] As one of the few Italian Americans to sit on the Massachusetts bench declared during a congressional hearing: "We protest against a policy which radically changes the rules of neutrality to the disadvantage of one belligerent—Italy."[28]

Unlike Italian-Jewish conflict in New York following the formation of the Rome-Berlin Axis in 1937 and the promulgation of Mussolini's anti-Semitic Decrees in 1936, Italian-Jewish animosities were limited in Boston. In October 1938, *La Notizia* launched a scurrilous attack on Jews to justify Mussolini's anti-Semitic decrees.[29] Similarly, the *Italian News* attacked the *Jewish Advocate* in a front-page editorial for promoting propaganda against Mussolini in Boston.[30] But anti-Semitism was not a central issue for Boston's Italian press. Indeed, Italian-Jewish antipathies never approached those of New York where in 1939 the Sons of Italy Grand Lodge distributed a circular pointing out that "anti-Semitism in Europe, unfortunately, has had repercussions in America, particularly in the City and State of New York, causing a spirit of hatred between Italians and Jews that can only culminate in a daily struggle."[31] The residential and economic segregation of the Italians in the West End, North End, and Esst Boston and Jews in Roxbury and Dorchester probably lessened explicit conflict in the Hub. Tensions and resentments lingered, however.[32]

College professors, internationalists, Anglophiles, and communists repeatedly received abusive treatment in Boston's Italian press.[33] In many cases, international issues heightened domestic dissatisfaction with life in Boston and in the United States. The effects of Italian prejudice took its toll on the inhabitants of Boston's West End, the North End, and East Boston.[34] The *Gazzetta del Massachusetts* epitomized the rampant cynicism and frustration felt by many Boston Italians when it bluntly described the North End "as a dumping ground of all the refuse of the City of Boston...."[35] The *Italian News* perceived its central role in the community as one of defending the honor of Italian culture and values.[36] International issues and events, therefore, served as catalysts for the articulation of ethnic grievances and the search for a meaningful Italian American ethnic identity.

The domestic and international achievements of Mussolini's Italy became an important dimension of an Italian American identity.[37] The isolation of Italian Americans from mainstream American culture made Mussolini's accomplishments all the more appealing. In Boston, rampant discrimination exacerbated anxieties and tensions within their neighborhoods. Just as Italians were subordinated to the Irish in the church and politics, they felt the sting of Irish control of federal relief funds. Irish sections received 82 percent of the initial sixty-three hundred apartments of federally funded housing projects while only 16 percent went to Italian neighborhoods. Moreover, Italian residents of the North End faced discrimination in the allocation of Works Project Administration (WPA) jobs receiving less than half the positions for which they were eligible. Conversely, the Irish received more than 14 percent of their fair share of WPA positions.[38] Therefore, faced with the highest unemployment rates in Boston, unsatisfactory patterns of upward mobility, deteriorating neighborhoods, and job discrimination, Italians turned to Italy for solace during the 1930s. Consequently, the Italian Americans' support for fascism was less an explicit political choice than an attempt to redefine their historical status in the United States.

In this social, psychological, and cultural environment no event was more important to Italian American self-identity than the Italo-Ethiopian War. John Diggins described it as a "sustained catharsis."[39] In Boston the Italian invasion of Ethiopia brought to the surface long-suppressed frustrations, ushering in a period of sporadic ethnic conflict. Mussolini received the widespread approval of Boston's Italian community. The Italian press forcefully supported the domestic and international consequences of fascism in Italy.[40] Support for the Benito Mussolini Club flourished while membership in the anti-Mussolini Mazzini Society and the Lincoln Italian Club was limited.[41] Political, socioeconomic, and cultural frustrations with life in Boston contrasted sharply with Italian victories in Ethiopia and contributed to a heightened awareness of Italian identity in Boston. Preoccupation with Italy's standing in the world provided Boston Italians with tangible evidence of their self-worth. Culturally isolated and geographically removed from the rest of Boston, the Italian-Ethiopian conflict allowed Boston's Italians to assert the validity of their ethnic inheritance. Moreover, the concern generated by the war in Africa illustrated the role of transnational ties in helping to shape an Italian American world view. The *Gazzetta del Massachusetts* reflected the importance that Boston's Italians attached to the international achievements of Italy when it observed: "Italian is the language of Italy, a country of increasing importance in world affairs."[42]

As 1939 came to a close, the support accorded Mussolini by Boston's Italian community exacerbated already strained intergroup relations. The immediate effects of the impact of the international system resulted in heightened tensions between Italians and Blacks and, to a lesser extent, Italians and Jews.

From a broader perspective, however, those patterns of ethnic conflict in Boston constituted a search for a meaningful Italian American identity. The outburst of ethnic conflict in Boston was a complex process that fused together elements of the Italian American scene with the rapidly deteriorating international system of the last years of the 1930s. The setting of Boston's Italian community was an important factor in defining the specific form that ethnic conflict would assume. Undoubtedly, the institutional completeness of Italian Boston—its high degree of spatial segregation and low rates of upward socioeconomic mobility, its political isolation, and its cultural alienation—influenced the way that Boston's Italian community reacted to ongoing international events. But the interactions between the international system and the domestic scene of the 1930s also revealed much about the strength of ethnic bonds. Boston's Italians were often one or two generations removed from the Italian homeland; yet the power of affective ties with Italy remained strong. It is from this perspective that ethnic conflict must be understood as the logical extension of the search for a meaningful Italian American identity.

Boston's Italians were not alone in their preoccupation with ongoing international issues and events to be sure. Irish concern with anti-communism and isolationism and an equally forceful Jewish concern with Zionism and anti-Semitism amplified patterns of ethnic conflict in Boston.

IN PURSUIT OF LIBERALISM: BOSTON'S JEWS, ETHNIC CONFLICT, AND THE INTERNATIONAL SYSTEM

Just as Boston's Irish and Italians struggled to establish meaningful ethnic identities in the turbulent years of the 1930s, Boston's Jewish community confronted unprecedented challenges. From an international perspective, the rise of the Third Reich, fascism, and new and horrifying waves of European anti-Semitism raised doubts about the survival of the Jewish people. In the United States, anti-Semitism, isolationism, and xenophobia presented American Jews with difficult issues about their place in America. Unquestionably, the intrusion of international issues and events played a significant role in shaping Jewish ethnicity.

In Boston, as in New York and Chicago, distinctive political, socioeconomic, and cultural institutions defined the precise manifestations that Jewish ethnicity assumed. Unlike the defensiveness and rancor of Irish Boston and the intense bitterness and frustration apparent in Italian neighborhoods, the Hub's Jewish community struggled to assert a liberal ethos. Whereas Boston's Italians greeted the international events of the 1930s as a catharsis and the Irish vented their frustrations through muted conflict, the Jewish response to the international system was often more complex.

The 1930s were years of intense transitions for Boston's Jews. Political, economic, and social institutions were changing rapidly within the Jewish community. These changes inevitably were reflected in Jewish outlooks in Boston. Amid the changing structure of the community, the force of the international system dramatically heightened a historic sense of ethnicity. Thus rising ethnic tensions in Boston (Italian chauvinisms, Irish anti-Semitism, and Italian Irish isolationism) often strained evolving Jewish identities, occasionally threatening the realization of liberal ideals. The last years of the 1930s in particular constituted a watershed in the development of Jewish ethnicity in Boston. Ultimately, the tensions between a liberal ethos and ethnic ties gave rise to a Jewish identity embracing a liberalism and a communalism that the onslaught of explicit Irish anti-Semitism in the 1940s did not destroy. This demonstrated the flexibility and resilience of ethnicity. Although American Jews have not been notably united, the force of the international system lessened divisions within Boston's Jewish community. Unquestionably, the issues and events of the 1930s heightened a sense of peoplehood in Boston's Jewish neighborhoods.

Two issues in particular directly intruded in the Hub's Jewish enclaves. One concerned the waves of anti-Semitism and fascism that swept across Europe in the 1930s. The other was the search by Zionists for a permanent solution to the worldwide persecution of Jews. The Jewish response to Zionism and anti-Semitism epitomized the interplay between the international system and ethnicity in Boston.

As the international environment progressively deteriorated in the 1930s, support for Zionism dramatically increased in Boston after 1936.[43] In 1938, when the British government announced its intention of repudiating the Balfour Declaration, thus ending any commitment to the establishment of a Jewish national state in Palestine, Boston's Jewish community reacted with outrage.[44] Again in 1939, British foreign policy created an uproar in the Jewish community. At that time the United Kingdom released a White Paper calling for the creation of an Arab State in Palestine with a Jewish population stabilized at one-third of the proposed country's total size. The *Jewish Advocate* vowed "that the Jews will never yield to Arab subjugation and we will never be party to this great betrayal."[45] When Chaim Weizman, president of the World

Zionist Organization, arrived in Boston in 1940, Boston's Jewish community greeted him with acclaim. There was a marked proliferation of organizations devoted to Palestine in Boston: the American Jewish Joint Distributing Committee, the United Palestine Appeal for Refugees, and the Boston Refugee Committee.[46] The community's most influential leaders—Louis Kirstein, Felix Frankfurter, Ben Selekman, David Niles, Rabbi Harry Levi—were active in both the Zionist cause and the refugee problem.[47]

Zionism exerted an impact on Boston's Jewish community that transcended financial and moral support for Zionist organizations, however. Fundamentally, Zionism constituted a solution to the dilemma of worldwide anti-Semitism for future generations. "Jews can be good and loyal and faithful citizens of whatever country in which they dwell, but once they are questioned, once their enemies rise against them, only Palestine can still assure and guarantee them the rights and privileges of human beings. . . ." The *Jewish Advocate* observed: "It [Zionism] is an affirmative and positive movement, drawing its inspiration from faith, hope, and ambition rather than from despair and defeat. . . . There is one simple answer; there is no substitute for Palestine."[48] The issue of Zionism transcended support for a state of Palestine, however. It went to the heart of ethnic attachments—the depth and intensity of a sense of peoplehood. "It is a revitalizing and re-energizing force in the life of a Jew; it is a living contact with one's own people. . . . The richness, the spiritual content of Zionism, the fullness of its message, should be brought home to every congregation member." The *Jewish Advocate* concluded: "Not mere acceptance, but actual participation in Zionist work will bring new meaning and understanding to organized Jewish life which has been lacking."[49]

Second, Zionism evoked a theme of renewal and regeneration in the face of intense persecution in the life of the Jewish people. "Palestine has taken them from a living grave in Germany and brought them back to life."[50] The theme of regeneration affirmed the link to a historical religious past that strengthened ethnic bonds, thereby providing pychological comfort in a time of intense emotional and spiritual distress. Indeed, Zionism's emphasis on renewal was yet another expression of secular messianism—an outlook firmly rooted in Jewish culture.

Finally, Zionism constituted an ultimate solution to the diaspora.

In so doing, Zionism gave meaning to historic sacrifices. Thus Zionism served to link the richness of the Jewish past to the promise of a more hopeful future. "The new life and the spirit will originate with us in the Diaspora, and will but find its reflection in Palestine. From within us will spring the joy, the spontaneity, the understanding, which, frustrated for centuries, will find reflection in Eretz Israel."[51]

Cognizance of anti-Semitism and fascism, like the appeal of Zionism, illustrated the interaction between the international arena and ethnicity in Boston. Specifically, the intensifying Nazi persecution of the Jews in Germany and the spread of organized anti-Semitism throughout Europe sensitized Boston's Jewish community to the threat of anti-Semitism and fascism in the United States. The *Jewish Advocate* played a significant role in directing attention to the problems created by anti-Semitism and fascism. The *Advocate* took a decidedly activist stance in community affairs. Its editors perceived their role as "reflecting community activities, interpreting and explaining events."[52] Not surprisingly, the *Advocate* was engrossed by events in Europe. Its coverage of international events, particularly anti-Semitism, was generally responsible and restrained in marked contrast to the international coverage of Boston's remaining ethnic press: the *Boston Pilot*, the *Gazzetta del Massachusetts*, and the *Italian News*. "As Jews we cannot disassociate ourselves from what is happening in Germany," the *Advocate* explained. "Our people are the victims of a form of government which makes no pretense of its hatred and which can be open to no misunderstanding, for anti-Semitism is their policy by admission and by law."[53] The principal thrust of the *Advocate's* reporting covered incidents of anti-Semitism throughout Europe. Therefore, it was significant that anti-Semitism came to be seen not as an isolated series of events but as a single tidal wave threatening world Jewry with ultimate destruction. This perspective stood in diametrical opposition to the Irish view of communist insurgence.

There are some who like to speak of the "Red Menace" sweeping over Europe and cry out that Communism is engulfing the world. It is apparent that the real menace is Fascism. The map of Europe only too well demonstrates the danger. Italy and Germany are already in the iron clutch; Spain struggles to free itself from the grasp; France's Leftist government is none too secure from attacks by the powerful fascist groups, Nazism is an even more threatening force in Austria....Even sturdy Britain faces street riots and open threats against the government on the part of Oswald Mosley and his troops.[54]

With the Italian embrace of anti-Semitism in 1937 and 1938, the *Advocate* concluded that Italy proved the inherent anti-Semitism of fascism for those who had previously doubted it.[55] Throughout the world, the specter of fascist victories—in Germany, Spain, Italy—haunted Boston's Jewish community. The menace of anti-Semitism reinforced the salience of ethnic identity. "So terrific are the forces arrayed against us, not only in Germany, but in all of Central Europe, that no Jew dare turn a deaf ear to the pitiful cry of his unfortunate brethren. Traitor indeed is he who forsakes the cause in his hour of direct need! In every city and town and hamlet Jews must stand together as they have never done before."[56] The realization that anti-Semitism was an omnipresent force in the last years of the 1930s invariably heightened intergroup tensions in Boston. Ethnic conflict resulted. Several incidents illustrated escalating patterns of group conflict in Boston.

The dismissal of a group of 168 young Jewish women from the WPA library reclassification project in Boston during the spring of 1936 resulted in the first explicit manifestations of heightening tensions in Jewish neighborhoods. The Jewish community greeted the news of the mass firings with outrage. City Councilor Charles I. Taylor, representing Jewish Ward 14, decried the introduction of such blatant "racial prejudice" into Boston.[57] Again in 1938, Councilor Taylor rose in City Hall to protest discrimination in another WPA project. "I dislike very much to introduce any order which has reference to racial prejudice," Taylor pointed out, "but it makes my blood boil to think that in a democratic city and in a democratic country we should be subjected to any such prejudice."[58] Indeed, Irish discrimination against Jews and Italians was rampant in a number of federally funded programs throughout the 1930s.[59]

But it was the impact of the international environment that brought latent ethnic animosities to a head in Boston. When a

special Massachusetts commission investigating anti-Semitic organizations in the Bay State reported that organized anti-Semitic
groups were active in Massachusetts, an editorial in the *Advocate*
complained: "For the past half dozen years we have consistently
commented on the agitation which was being carried on by various
local groups, to which many replied that we were merely looking
for something that didn't exist."[60] By far the most significant dimensions of Jewish ethnic conflict resulted from the substantial
Coughlinite movement in Boston's Irish neighborhoods. Here
Boston's Jews confronted undeniable proof of the internationalism
of fascism, anti-Semitism, and violence.

Initially, Coughlin was belittled in the pages of the *Advocate*. It
was not difficult to ridicule the ignorance and stupidity of the radio
priest's rhetoric. As tensions mounted, the Hub's Jewish community began to worry about the rise of anti-Semitism in South Boston,
Roxbury, and Dorchester. As early as June 1936, the *Advocate*
pointed out that "gangs" were attacking Jews near Irish neighborhoods in Roxbury.[61] In August 1936, Father Coughlin began to release the full fury of his anti-Semitic invective at the Union party's
nominating convention in Cleveland. The *Advocate* warned its
readers of the radio priest's deadly game.[62] Moreover, Jews tended
to view Irish support of Father Coughlin as veiled manifestations of
anti-Semitism in Boston. "The mounting crescendo of his anti-
Semitic utterances are definite causes for alarm," the *Advocate*
warned. "The increasing severity of his criticisms of the Jew, his
more and more frequent outspoken condemnation of our people is
unquestionably part of a planned campaign moving toward a
definite culmination."

> Father Coughlin is playing a dangerous game on human emotions.
> His smooth tongue and oily voice are weapons of one who is guilty
> of inciting man against man—a crime against his own God. And
> there are millions—who knows how many—who listen to him and
> drink in his words....
> It is not fear that motivates us so much as indignation. That this
> man should continue to wield power, should continue to mold the
> opinions of his followers along his own twisted and misshapen chan-
> nels, is to us an insult to America. There is no longer any sham in all
> this; Coughlin has dropped the curtains, has stepped forth from his

pseudo-friendship and has emerged, in his own words, as a challenger to the Jew.[63]

Indeed, Father Coughlin cast a ubiquitous and menacing shadow over Boston's Jewish community. Anti-Semitism, both real and imagined, strained relations between the Hub's Jewish and Irish communities. In 1937 the local chapter of the Anti-Defamation League shrilly demanded that the Boston School Committee remove the *Merchant of Venice* from the city's mandatory reading list.[64] The *Advocate* vigorously endorsed this move, arguing that Shakespeare's portrait of Shylock was a concession and appeal to the anti-Semitism of his time.[65]

A number of incidents of ethnic street violence reinforced Jewish perceptions of anti-Semitism in Boston. The *Advocate* reported the repeated occurrences of "organized" attacks on Jewish youths in the Franklin Park section of Roxbury-Mattapan. The report noted that gangs were coming from Irish neighborhoods in Hyde Park.[66] Boston's Jews threw the weight of their communal institutions against these domestic manifestations of anti-Semitism. The American Jewish Congress, the Anti-Defamation League, the Jewish People's Committee (the voice of Jewish labor in Boston), and Jewish War Veterans of America campaigned vigorously to eliminate the physical and verbal harassment of Jews. In fact, the community mobilized its resources so vigorously to combat fascism and anti-Semitism in the Hub that the *Advocate* complained of "needless duplication" of energies and "fragmentation" of resources.[67] Undoubtedly, the perception of anti-Semitic and quasi-fascist inroads in Boston strengthened the salience of communal bonds. A social worker at Hecht House illustrated a heightened sense of ethnicity based on the interaction of domestic and international events when he reported:

> We are in the midst of a large Jewish community. Many of our boys and girls are grandchildren of immigrants. Fascism has disrupted the world. Anti-Semitism is threatening America. It is difficult for Jewish boys and girls to enter many colleges and professional schools. Jobs are scarce for everyone. Some lines of endeavor are entirely closed to Jews. There is an added problem of caring for Jewish refugees from Central Europe.[68]

By 1939 the editors of the *Advocate* reported that the worldwide manifestations of fascism and anti-Semitism had increased the willingness of Boston's Jews to support financially Jewish organizations in the Hub.[69]

Even amid a rising defensiveness via the mobilization of communal institutions to combat anti-Semitism, the leadership of Boston's Jewish community never completely abandoned a self-conscious pursuit of liberal ideals. This ethnic orientation, exemplified in political, socioeconomic, and cultural institutions, contrasted dramatically with those of Irish and Italian Boston. Perhaps it was the worldwide specter of fanaticism and hate that tempered outbursts of indignation in Jewish Boston. This restraint further distinguished Boston's Jews from the profascism that seized the Italian North End or the incidents of anti-Semitism that occurred in Irish neighborhoods.

Repeatedly, communal elites tried to make sense out of the insanity of world events. The triumph of Nazism, the spread of fascism, the quest for a Jewish state in Palestine, the tangible menace of anti-Semitism in the Hub, weighed heavily on the mind and heart of Jewish Boston. "Is Civilization Worth Saving?" the *Advocate* asked. "No matter where we turn in this world today, we find the forces of reaction, superstition, medievalism and ignorance gaining the ascendant power. The few liberals and intellectuals seem to be waging a constantly losing fight to save a world that doesn't want to be saved."[70] Bordering on despair, the *Advocate* acutely recognized the dilemma that confronted persecuted minorities in the 1930s. The resulting tensions between the rights of a minority and the tyranny of the majority threatened to overwhelm a commitment to democratic ideals.[71] Ultimately, the *Advocate* discovered in historic Jewish messianism a partial answer to the dilemma of liberal political aspirations in a chaotic world. "Is civilization worth saving? Should we continue our battle, or should we withdraw to an intellectual ghetto, as it were, and let the world sweep on to its destruction? Can we withdraw to the cloister, or must we continue our efforts to propagate morality and understanding," the *Advocate* asked. "This, perhaps, is what might be called the mission of Israel, and it might properly be called the mission of all 'the remnant,' the liberals and the intellectuals."[72] The difficulties of developing a constructive Jewish attitude to democratic ideals and

values preoccupied other communitywide institutions. The huge
fund-raising drives of the Associated Jewish Philanthropies hammered home the theme of a special Jewish commitment to American socioeconomic and political values.[73] At Hecht Neighborhood
House, its staff worried about how they could reinforce the importance of democratic aspirations in the face of worldwide anti-
Semitism. Each staff member sought to emphasize the compatibility of Judaism with American ideals. "My philosophy accepts the
theory of the rights of minorities to maintain themselves and contribute diverse culture to many other cultures," the director explained. "As far as modern anti-Semitism is concerned, I believe the
cause to be economic—that the Jews are used as scapegoats to
divert the thoughts of oppressed peoples from their difficulties."
She continued:

> The cure, I believe, is found in Jews joining with the non-Jews in all
> liberal movements—unobstrusively and generously—in order that
> the political and economic democracy be attained. The hope lies
> through the education of a new generation in tolerance and in wish-
> ing for economic equality. Continuously, it is brought home to the
> thinking American Jew that he is a Jew. Anti-Semitism is rampant in
> Europe and is making inroads in this hemisphere. Therefore, it is es-
> sential that every Jew think through the problem and come to a con-
> clusion which makes it possible for him to find inner peace and peace
> with his environment.[74]

Similarly, another staff member saw in the impact of the deteriorating international system the necessity of a rededication to Jewish
ethnic values and American life. He argued that the spread of
totalitarianism could be combated only through the practice of
democracy "to its fullest extent and according to its broadest definitions." The staff believed that Hecht House must emphasize the
necessity of active involvement in all phases of the political process. The specter of spreading European anti-Semitism in the 1930s
played a critical role in this philosophy. "Let us frankly open up the
problem of social action to our boys and girls. If we do not, we are
derelict in our duty. We cannot and dare not take social injustice
passively. The people of Germany and Italy did that. We know too
well the results."[75]

On a number of occasions, Jews gave tangible expression to their liberal ecumenical aspirations. The *Advocate* reminded its readers that Catholics experienced intense religious persecution in Mexico, Spain, and Germany.[76] "The situation in Spain, for example, has given rise to many false conceptions regarding the stand of the Catholic Church on Fascism," the editors of the *Advocate* declared. "While local conditions may align Catholics on one side or the other, the Church can never be considered an ally of the Nazi Fascist movement which it is fighting in Germany."[77] In a spectacular gesture of goodwill the United Jewish Appeal gave two hundred and fifty thousand dollars in 1939 to the Catholic church as a memorial to the late Pope Pius XI. But a deteriorating international environment and heightening tensions in Boston—Irish anti-Semitism and Italian philofascism, for example—threatened the full realization of liberal ideals.

Indeed, European anti-Semitism strained relations between Jews and Irish to the breaking point. By far the main areas of conflict centered on Catholic support for fascism in Spain and Portugal and Irish tolerance of Coughlinism in the Hub. The insensitivities of Irish and Italians were all the more intolerable in the face of European anti-Semitism, "this unending procession of suffering and distress of the innocent young and old."[78] In particular, the leadership of Boston's Jewish community could not understand the reluctance of the Catholic church formally to condemn the Nazi reign of terror in 1935, 1936, and 1937.[79] The *Advocate* publicly decried the moral insensitivities of Roman Catholicism to anti-Semitism. On Easter Sunday, April 9, 1938, the *Advocate* published on its front page, "An Epistle" to Pope Pius XI:

> Your Holiness, speak out to the world in protest and condemnation, and rally the faithful of the Roman Catholic Church to an unyielding and open opposition to tyrannical dictatorships, whether under the red flag or the brown. Issue a call for united action by all lovers of peace and goodwill among men. Ask the members of your great church to preach from every pulpit the message of tolerance and brotherhood and neighborliness which the Founder of Christianity preached. Point a finger of denunciation at those who challenge religion and urge upon Catholics everywhere to declare a moral, spiritual and economic boycott of the enemies of faith.

The *Advocate* reminded the pope that the turmoil in Mexico ". . . is not solely a Catholic issue any more than the problem in Germany is a Jewish one." It called upon Pius XI to lead a united war of Protestants, Catholics, and Jews "in combating the spread of dangerous ideologies in our times and among our rising generations." The *Advocate* concluded by declaring that "Every man of humility, of respect, understanding, and love of God is prepared to join with you in a Twentieth Century Crusade to save for our posterity the ideals and concepts by which men are guided to lives of righteousness, justice and purity."[80]

The *Advocate* received a torrent of mail in response to its "Epistle to the Pope." Its analysis of the mail confirmed the heightening tensions within Boston's Jewish community. It pointed out that the mail could be divided into two classifications. There were those of all faiths who praised the "Epistle." "Many felt that our call was an historic and unprecedented platform on which all religions could unite for the greater cause which was common to all."[81] On the other hand, the *Advocate* labeled those who opposed the "Epistle" as people "with anti-Semitic tendencies who seized the widespread publicity to write what they thought of Jews in general."[82] The reaction of the *Advocate* to the mail that disagreed with the "Epistle" revealed the salience of domestic and international events in the final years of the 1930s. It pointed out that some of the letters were vicious, "some contained veiled threats, some showed gross ignorance of a moronic level, and some were merely from cranks." It was the number of letters in the last category that most bothered the editors of the *Advocate*, however. "If there are so many cranks and misanthropes in this country who will sit down and voluntarily pen a letter to a Jewish newspaper about which they have read, one must wonder about the possible conditions which would ensue were such people to come to power."[83] Undoubtedly, the rise of Nazism in Germany and anti-Semitic activities in the United States were of grave concern to the editors of the *Advocate*.

Despite the Vatican's explicit condemnations of anti-Semitism in 1938 and 1939, and the generous memorial to Pope Pius XI provided by the United Jewish Appeal, doubts lingered about the sincerity of Irish Catholic opposition to anti-Semitism in Boston. The Boston Irish were in the midst of an antisubversive binge; the Boston City Council spent much of its time Red-baiting, the school committee articulated a shrill defensiveness, and the Irish members of the state legislature earnestly looked for communist inroads in Boston. Isolationism was pervasive in Boston's Irish and Italian communities as well. Moreover, both the Irish and Italians flirted with anti-Semitism. Indeed, it was the specter of Father Coughlin's supporters in South Boston, Roxbury, and Dorchester that heightened Jewish anxiety in Boston. "It is the Fascist sympathizers such as Father Coughlin and his ilk, who are bringing in the Jews as the bogey-man in order to break up any attempt on the part of this country to help the democracies in Europe," as one member of Boston's Jewish community pointed out. "It is surprising to know that in my talks with the Irish people, I find that 95 percent of them approve of Father Coughlin's attacks on the Jews. George Britt in the *Nation* also points out that it is the Irish rather than the Germans who are Coughlin's Storm Troopers."[84]

Irish support for Coughlin cast a menacing shadow over Boston's entire Jewish community. Cognizance of the horror of European anti-Semitism and the fear of greater anti-Semitic inroads in Boston further strained relations between Irish and Jews.[85] The *Advocate* fully concurred. It concluded that anti-Semitism was the "most basic fifth column activity in America."[86] The continued failure of the Catholic church formally to disavow Father Coughlin's activities infuriated Boston's Jews. "There are priests in America," the *Advocate* warned, "who need to be told that their faith does not preclude a respect for the religion of others."[87] When vandals desecrated a Jewish cemetery in New London, Connecticut, in late 1939, the *Advocate* stridently concluded that the ultimate responsibility for such actions rested on Christianity.[88] By the spring of 1940, the *Advocate* felt compelled to warn the Catholic church to silence or at least formally disavow Coughlin "if it did not wish its doctrine interpreted as a doctrine of hate and violence."[89] An official Catholic condemnation of Coughlin was not forthcoming. The decade concluded on an uneasy note, marked by heightened tensions and explicit antipathies. Mutual suspicions and bitterness characterized ethnic outlooks even in Boston's enlightened Jewish community. Unquestionably, the international system had strengthened the salience of ethnicity in the Hub. The various forms that ethnic conflict assumed depended on a number of factors, however.

Boston's Italians withdrew into their ethnic enclaves noticeably more disturbed with American life than before the Italo-Ethiopian War. Through their isolationism and their support for Italian foreign policy, Boston's Italians expressed long-suppressed bitterness and resentments. These hostilities were at the root of an Italian American world view. Mussolini's Ethiopian campaign was a catharsis for Boston's Italians but it did not solve their problems of adjustment to life in the United States. Indeed, Italian ethnicity in the last years of the 1930s constituted a search for meaningful Italian American identities. The search continued beyond the turbulent 1930s to be sure. Italian ethnic conflict illustrated the importance of the international system in helping to shape an ethnic outlook in the United States. The very transnational nature of Italian American identities in Boston demonstrated the fluidity of ethnicity as well as its emotional power. Italian ethnic conflict symbolized the problems inherent in Italian ancestry and American citizenship during the 1930s. Both the Italians and the Irish were isolationist and anticommunist as well as increasingly dissatisfied with the liberal cast of the New Deal. But even agreement on these issues failed to bridge ethnic differences—expressed in political, socioeconomic, and cultural terms—separating these communities. Irish and Italians were as suspicious of each other in the 1930s as in previous decades. The impact of the international system had forced these groups to turn inward, seeking in ethnicity some stability and reassurance in a chaotic world. The cultural isolation and atomization of Boston's Italians and Irish reinforced resentments and bitterness that in turn fueled ethnic conflict. The tragedy of the 1930s, therefore, was not in the increasing importance of Italian and Irish identities but the profoundly negative manifestations that they assumed.

The international system, too, influenced the form of Jewish ethnicity in Boston. Ethnic conflict did not seize Boston's Jewish neighborhoods with the same force as it did in the Italian North End or in Irish South Boston. The impact of the international system undoubtedly heightened a historic sense of ethnicity, but a number of specific factors tended to lessen the intensity of ethnic conflict. First, the institutional structure of the Jewish community limited the scope of ethnic hostilities. Resentments, frustrations, and bitterness were there, to be sure. The reality of European anti-Semitism and fascism made explicit manifestations of Irish and Italian anti-Semitism in Boston an abomination. Unlike much of the leadership in Italian and Irish communities, Boston's Jews tried to deal with the international and domestic problems of the 1930s in a positive fashion. Boston's Jews gave expression to a constructive self-identity through a number of men and institutions: community leaders such as Louis Kirstein, Ben Selekman, Rabbi Harry Levi, David Niles, the enlightened staff of Hecht House, the leadership of the *Advocate*, and the panoply of organizations allied with the Associated Jewish Philanthropies. In their cognizance of the international and domestic manifestations of anti-Semitism, they sought a reaffirmation of the integrity of the ethnic group and its compatibility with American values and ideals.

From a historical perspective, the final years of the 1930s constituted a period of immense transition in Boston's Jewish neighborhoods. The Jewish community was well on the way to achieving middle-class status—in wealth, education, and occupational mobility.[90] By mid-decade, old residential patterns gave way to strikingly altered ones. The Jewish community settled into the lower-middle-class and middle-class neighborhoods of Roxbury, Dorchester, and Mattapan.[91] Life along Dorchester's expansive Blue Hill Avenue contrasted greatly with the former overcrowded and deteriorating neighborhoods of Boston's West End. Even during the worst periods of the depression, there was at least the promise of a brighter future.[92]

There were discernible changes in Jewish political orientations. Residual support for Republican candidates for national office declined throughout the years of the 1930s. Boston's Jews increasingly responded to the social welfare policies of the New Deal.[93] Whereas the apogee of Irish and Italian support for the Democratic party came in 1928 with Al Smith's candidacy, F.D.R. received steadily increasing pluralities in Jewish neighborhoods throughout the

1930s and 1940s. Although Boston's Irish and Italians unquestionably supported the New Deal, there was a visible decrease in enthusiasm for F.D.R. personally.

Jewish reactions to the New Deal contrasted markedly with Irish and Italian outlooks. These differing perspectives were most evident in the personal ties that bound Boston's Jewish community to the New Deal. Indeed, the most articulate spokesmen for the New Deal in Boston were Jews—Niles, Frankfurter, Kirstein, A. Lincoln Filene, Selekman, and Rabbi Levi. These communal leaders differed from those leaders of Irish and Italian Boston in style and outlook. By 1936 Cardinal O'Connell, Senator Walsh, Governor Curley, Mario Renna, and a host of lesser lights looked upon the New Deal and its liberal "brain trusters" with considerable suspicion, much reservation, and increasing antipathy. In short, Jews embraced a political liberalism that further distinguished them from Irish and Italians.[94]

Indeed, Boston's rabbinates forcefully supported the social welfare objectives of the New Deal, seeing in them traditional Jewish cultural values. On October 1, 1935, Boston's rabbis called for a basic "reconstruction" of the American economic system. They argued ". . . that all enterprises that are essential to social life must be owned and controlled not by individuals and families but by society itself."[95]

Differences in political and social welfare values, therefore, differentiated Boston's Irish, Italian, and Jewish communities. Jews translated differences in style into outlooks that aimed at integration with the institutions of the host society. Ironically, this emphasis served only to reinforce the salience of distinctive Jewish cultural values in politics, culture, and socioeconomic concerns. There were tensions, of course, between the traditions of the ethnic group and the values of the host society, but Boston's Jewish leaders managed to cope very well with such strains. For example, in 1937 the *Christian Century* suggested that Jewish "exclusiveness" was responsible for the "Jewish problem" throughout the world. The *Christian Century* urged all Jews to assimilate to "American" standards as a means of "best following the spirit of democracy." The *Advocate* viewed such expressions of nativism with undisguised contempt. In its reply to the *Christian Century*, the *Advocate* reaffirmed the primacy of the ethnic group and support for traditional American political values. "It was always our belief that a system which demanded that minorities yield up their individuality and succumb entirely to the will of the majority was incompatible with democracy. We have always viewed democracy as a guarantor of personal liberties, for individuals and for groups."[96]

In essence, the impact of the international system confronted Boston's Jews with the challenge of a creative response to American ideals and values. Louis Kirstein suggested the essence of distinctive Jewish values when he described the role of the ethnic group. "...We belong to the Jewish group and most of us will make our contribution in these provinces, as members of the Jewish group and as members of no other. Some may attempt to escape that affiliation and still fewer escape it successfully but for most of us, that attachment is real, lasting, and embracing, whether we like it or not..."[97] That realization, Kirstein asserted, strengthened the contributions that Jews made to American life. Although a Jewish cultural inheritance was something more than a voluntary affiliation, it was by no means static, particularly in a period of increasing international tensions.[98]

Thus a recognition of the compatibility of American and Jewish values reinforced the primacy of the ethnic group for the leadership of Boston's Jewish community. Their self-conscious pursuit of liberalism illustrated the profound political, socioeconomic, cultural, and psychological transitions that were taking hold of Jewish Boston. Rather than retreating inward, Boston's Jews tried to deal constructively with the tensions between political ideals and international realities. This was clearly the case in social welfare matters—New Deal politics, involvement in the NAACP, and in dealing with Italian and Irish preoccupation with past and present grievances. Boston's Jews were striving to remove those barriers, physical as well as psychological, separating them from the Hub's progressive Brahmins and Yankees.[99]

The fuller test of Jewish ethnic identity and liberal values came in the first years of the 1940s. The imminence of American involvement in World War II and the onslaught of renewed anti-Semitism in Boston set the framework in which Jewish ethnic identities, no less than Irish and Italian, were further defined.

NOTES

1. John P. Diggins, *Mussolini and Fascism, The View from America* (Princeton: Princeton University Press, 1972), p. 51.

2. Barbara M. Soloman, *Ancestors and Immigrants, A Changing New England Tradition* (Cambridge: Harvard University Press, 1956), pp. 164-67; John Higham, *Strangers in the Land, Patterns of American Nativism 1860-1925* (New York: Atheneum, 1974), pp. 133-44, 149-57.

3. Diggins, *Mussolini and Fascism*, pp. 26-27, 78-79.

4. Ibid., pp. 76, 79; see also Ronald H. Bayor, *Neighbors in Conflict, The Irish, Germans, Jews, and Italians of New York City, 1929-1941* (Baltimore: Johns Hopkins University Press, 1978), p. 78.

5. Diggins suggests the central role that Mussolini played in the Italian American quest for self-esteem when he writes: "An unwelcome stranger in a sometimes hostile land, the Italian American looked almost desperately to his home country for personal solace and national identity." *Mussolini and Fascism*, p. 79.

6. Charles H. Trout, "Boston During the Great Depression 1928-1940" (Ph.D. diss., Columbia University 1972), p. 526.

7. Diggins, *Mussolini and Fascism*, p. 306.

8. For a discussion of Italian-Black conflicts in New York, see ibid., pp. 306-7.

9. *Gazzetta del Massachusetts*, 13 July 1935; 23 March 1935: "Americans who wish to understand the Italy-Abyssinian imbroglio—which is of international importance inasmuch as it is complicating the already chaotic European situation—would do well to think of it in the light of the Japan-China issue.

"Like China, Abyssinia is an independent power and like China, it is a hundred years behind the times. Italy, like Japan, is an up-to-date nation, which needs new territory. China possesses a wealth of mineral resources, which Japan wants—and Abyssinia possesses a wealth of gold which Italy wants.

"If Italy and Abyssinia fight, it seems inevitable that the latter will lose. Victorious Italy would then establish an Abyssinian protectorate—and reap the rich rewards."

10. Virtually every issue of the *Gazzetta del Massachusetts* hammered home this theme during the Italo-Ethiopian War.

11. William F. Whyte, *Street Corner Society, The Social Structure of an Italian Slum* (Chicago: Chicago University Press, 1943), p. 274.

12. *Gazzetta del Massachusetts,* 29 June 1935; 20 July 1935; 12 July 1935.

13. Ibid., 25 July 1936.

14. Ibid., 12 July 1935; Diggins, *Mussolini and Fascism,* p. 83.

15. Trout, "Boston During the Great Depression," p. 537; Diggins, *Mussolini and Fascism,* pp. 306-7.

16. Diggins, *Mussolini and Fascism,* p. 306.

17. W.E.B. Du Bois, "The Inter-Racial Implications of the Ethiopian Crisis, A Negro View," *Foreign Affairs* 14 (October 1935): 85, 88.

18. Diggins, *Mussolini and Fascism,* p. 311.

19. Trout, "Boston During the Great Depression," pp. 537-43; *Guardian,* 2 September 1939; 11 February 1939; 18 March 1939.

20. Diggins, *Mussolini and Fascism,* p. 310.

21. *Guardian,* 17 June 1939.

22. As Diggins observes: "To the American Negro nurtured for centuries in a morass of self-hate and shame at his African ancestry, the Ethiopian War signified the awakening of a viable political consciousness. Perhaps no other diplomatic event until the post-World War II movements of African independence inspired black men to a new sense of identity and commitment." *Mussolini and Fascism,* pp. 311-12.

23. Robert A. Devine, *The Illusion of Neutrality, Franklin D. Roosevelt and the Struggle Over the Arms Embargo* (Chicago: Quadrangle Press, 1962), pp. 159-61.

24. *Gazzetta del Massachusetts,* 21 December 1935.

25. Ibid., 14 December 1935.

26. Devine, *Illusion of Neutrality,* pp. 150-51.

27. *Gazzetta del Massachusetts,* 25 January 1936.

28. Devine, *Illusion of Neutrality,* p. 151.

29. *Jewish Advocate,* 28 October 1938.

30. *Italian News,* 13 January 1939.

31. Bayor, *Neighbors in Conflict,* p. 85.

32. Trout, "Boston During the Great Depression," pp. 526-27; *Italian News,* 14 April 1939.

33. For anticommunism see: *Gazzetta del Massachusetts,* 11 May 1935; 14 September 1935; 24 January 1936; 14 March 1936; 15 August 1936; 28 November 1936; 5 June 1937; 2 October 1938; 27 September 1939; 20 April 1940; supporting American neutrality and isolationism: 20 April 1935; 1 February 1936; 8 August 1936; 20 May 1939; 7 October 1939; 28 October 1939; 4 November 1939.

34. Trout, "Boston During the Great Depression," p. 526.

35. *Gazzetta del Massachusetts*, 12 January 1935.

36. *Italian News*, 10 March 1939.

37. Diggins, *Mussolini and Fascism*, p. 78; Bayor, *Neighborhoods in Conflict*, p. 78.

38. Trout, "Boston During the Great Depression," pp. 526, 630, 638.

39. Diggins, *Mussolini and Fascism*, p. 302.

40. *Gazzetta del Massachusetts*, 12 November 1938.

41. Trout, "Boston During the Great Depression," p. 527.

42. *Gazzetta del Massachusetts*, 20 April 1935.

43. *Jewish Advocate*, 25 June 1937.

44. Ibid., 14 October 1938; 21 October 1938.

45. Ibid., 21 October 1938.

46. Ibid., 20 January 1939.

47. Trout, "Boston During the Great Depression," p. 546; Louis E. Kirstein Papers, Baker Library, Harvard University, Cambridge, Massachusetts, document the extreme efforts that Kirstein, Niles, and Frankfurter undertook on behalf of Jewish refugees throughout the world.

48. *Jewish Advocate*, 4 February 1938.

49. Ibid., 3 January 1936.

50. Ibid., 15 January 1935.

51. Ibid., 6 March 1936.

52. Ibid., 29 October 1937.

53. Ibid., 23 July 1935.

54. Ibid., 31 July 1936.

55. Ibid., 1 January 1936.

56. Ibid., 8 May 1936.

57. Ibid., 26 May 1936; 29 May 1936.

58. Boston, Mass., *Report of the Proceedings of the City Council of the City of Boston*, February 28, 1938, p. 86 (hereafter cited as *City Council Proceedings*).

59. Trout, "Boston During the Great Depression," pp. 630-38.

60. *Jewish Advocate*, 15 January 1935.

61. Ibid., 30 June 1936.

62. Ibid., 28 August 1936.

63. Ibid., 18 August 1936.

64. Ibid., 26 June 1937.

65. Ibid.

66. Ibid., 6 May 1938.

67. Ibid., 4 March 1938.

68. Papers of Hecht Neighborhood House, American Jewish Historical Society, Waltham, Massachusetts.

69. *Jewish Advocate*, 4 March 1938; 8 April 1938.

70. Ibid., 20 March 1936.

71. Cognizance of the transnational effects of anti-Semitism characterized this perspective. "Nazism is not an unexplainable phenomenon. It is an outgrowth of the very conditions we may see around us. People who brush by us in the streets, endowed by nature with inferior intellects, and granted by our constitution equal rights, are likely material for a similar movement. The indifference of the masses, their rejection of that which is above their comprehension, their first belief in shadows and delusions, makes preaching thankless and reform hopeless." Ibid., 20 March 1936.

72. Ibid.

73. Ibid., 4 October 1935. In fact, the theme of communal solidarity and democratic values appeared in every Associated Jewish Philanthropies campaign. The *Jewish Advocate* recorded this outlook every October.

74. Papers of Hecht Neighborhood House.

75. Ibid.

76. *Jewish Advocate*, 26 November 1935; 3 December 1937. "Inevitably there must be competitions between social groups but these need not be destructive or lead to hostility," 7 June 1935. Moreover, the Kirstein Papers, Case 5, throw considerable light on Jewish liberalism in Boston. The private letters exchanged between Louis Kirstein and William Cardinal O'Connell are most revealing in this respect.

77. *Jewish Advocate*, 3 December 1937.

78. Louis Kirstein, Speech, April 21, 1939, Louis E. Kirstein Papers.

79. *Jewish Advocate*, 14 February 1936. Pope Pius XI formally condemned fascism in his encyclical *Noi Appimo Pesogno* in 1938. The gift of two hundred and fifty thousand dollars in memory of Pius XI suggests the great relief with which American Jews greeted the Vatican's frequent expression of contempt for fascism and Nazism in 1938 and 1939.

80. Ibid., 15 April 1938.

81. Ibid., 22 April 1938.

82. Ibid.

83. Ibid.

84. Ibid., 5 May 1939.

85. "Report on Activities for the Year 1938-39," Papers of Hecht Neighborhood House.

86. *Jewish Advocate*, 15 March 1940; 31 May 1940.

87. Ibid., 6 October 1939.

88. Ibid., 27 October 1939.

89. Ibid., 15 March 1940; 31 May 1940.

90. For more extensive data on Jewish rates of socioeconomic mobility, see chapter 2.

91. "Annual Report, October 1, 1939-October 1, 1940," Papers of Hecht Neighborhood House.

92. Trout, "Boston During the Great Depression," p. 545.

93. Ibid., pp. 545-46.

94. Ibid., pp. 545-47.

95. Ibid., p. 546.

96. *Jewish Advocate*, 9 July 1937.

97. Louis Kirstein, "Jewish Speeches," Louis E. Kirstein Papers.

98. A staff member of Hecht House suggested a similar perspective in explaining her philosophy of Jewish life: "The word, Judaism, is not synonymous with Jewish religion. Judaism is something more; it is the sum total of the product of the Jewish consciousness, of the Jewish mind and of the Jewish soul. Judaism is something more than a mere system of beliefs; it is the essence of a living tradition; it is the civilization of the Jewish people. Judaism is the product of Jewish experience, of their culture, their literature, their philosophy, their ethics, their beliefs, their morals, and their folk ways. To separate the Jew from Judaism is to separate the organism from its true environment. The Jew should be well-informed concerning his cultural heritage. The poorly informed Jew thinks that the Jews today observe and believe in the same fashion as they did long ago in their national home in Palestine, which is not so. Any person who has thought of the Jewish life and Jewish teaching knows that there is, and always has been, a living growth and development in Jewish traditions." Papers of Hecht Neighborhood House.

99. Trout, "Boston During the Great Depression," p. 544.

5

International Politics and Ethnic Conflict in Boston: The War Years, 1940-1944

The intensity of ethnic conflict in Boston escalated as American involvement in World War II approached. The interaction between the international environment and Boston's Irish, Italians, and Jews brought to a climax several patterns of ethnic conflict that had been established in the latter years of the 1930s.

THE COMING OF WORLD WAR II

The Jews

"This report is being written on a black day in human destiny. The Germans are twelve miles from Paris. Pacificism has made its way in this country and now in the face of rampant oppression, people must readjust their thinking," wrote the executive director of the Hecht Neighborhood House on June 12, 1940.[1] She keenly perceived the impact of international events on Boston's Jewish community, particularly its youth. The imminence of World War II, anti-Semitism, and the salience of ethnic identities confused young people in Boston's Jewish community. Not surprisingly, the director worried about how these youth would reconcile democracy to the chaos of the world.

Most of the young people at Hecht House agree that all aid—short
of going to war—must be given the Allies. However, they know
"short of war" is no promise and they are reconciled to fighting.
There are also young people—and these are the most articulate and
the best informed as to social issues—who maintain that the United
States should not enter the war. They continuously talk of mistakes
made by the Allies and question the kind of a peace that will follow
the war in case of an Allied victory. However, events have moved so
fast that all we can say is that Youth is confused today about world
issues. They are more than ever desirous of democracy while ques-
tioning its efficiency in the world set-up of the present.[2]

Through their work at Hecht House, the staff reaffirmed a continuing commitment to American political values and a Jewish way of
life. However, the turbulent international system placed much
stress on the ultimate meaning of Jewish ethnicity.

Not only do we believe our young people should be prepared to
function in a democracy, but because they are Jewish, they should
understand their position as a minority group in that democracy.
And because that minority group has been and is still a persecuted
group, they must understand the positive values of Judaism—that
Judaism itself is based on democratic concepts and can exist only in a
democracy. Individually they must understand, accept and honor
their Judaism.[3]

A commitment to democratic values and ideals was one of the principal contributions that Boston's Jews made to the Hub and American life during the 1940s. Despite heightened tensions in the closing
years of the 1930s, the leaders of Boston's Jewish community refused
to reject liberal ideals.

The coming of World War II was a seminal event in the life of
Jewish neighborhoods. The struggle for Nazi mastery of Europe
symbolized the imminence of the forces of tyranny, intolerance,
and hate threatening to overwhelm the Jewish people throughout
the world. The impact of the international system promoted two
discernible trends in Boston's Jewish community. First, it heightened
a sense of Jewish identity. Second, the chaos of the international
system solidified a Jewish commitment to political liberalism. These
trends in Jewish Boston increased the gulf separating Jewish neigh-

borhoods from those of Irish and Italians. The outbursts of anti-Semitism in Boston between 1942 and 1944 attest to the further atomization of the city's ethnic groups in the 1940s.

Traditionally, American Jews have not been notably united. Even in 1940 the *Jewish Advocate* candidly admitted that "American Jewry does not share a common unanimity on events in Europe."[4] Several factors lessened divisive currents within Boston, however. The close-knit institutional structure of Boston's Jewish community strengthened ethnic ties in Jewish neighborhoods. The years of depression followed by a deteriorating international system in the 1930s facilitated the political, socioeconomic, and cultural mobilization of the community. Demographic factors also played a significant role. The relatively small size of Jewish Boston compared with those large and diversified communities in New York and Chicago fostered the strengthening of communal attachments. Moreover, Boston's Jews lived in close proximity to each other in neighborhoods of "remarkable solidarity."[5] Jewish sections of Roxbury, Dorchester, and Mattapan withstood the "economic ravages" of the depression far better than Irish and Italian enclaves.[6] But it was the direct impact of the international system on Jewish neighborhoods that fully resulted in a heightened sense of ethnic identity. The *Jewish Advocate* expressed this sense of peoplehood transcending national boundaries when it declared: "The Jews of the United States have arisen with heartening unanimity to help Britain in her hour of trial. The wholesale bombing of helpless civilians, which has characterized Nazi warfare, has made the British Isles a bastion not alone of the British Commonwealth but of American democracy as well."[7] With increasing intensity the Jewish community focused its attention on the international arena. The Battle of Britain transfixed Boston's Jews. It symbolized more than any other event of 1940 the essential interdependence of all mankind in the face of the Nazi Holocaust. "Upon the outcome of the battle depends the fate of our nation, the lives of our population, the happiness and security of future generations," the *Jewish Advocate* declared. "Neutral in deed and act, in accordance with the policy of our government, there is hardly an American worthy of the name who does not admit to a deep and fervent sympathy for the British cause, linked as it is so closely with our own."[8]

Boston's Jews reintensified their efforts on behalf of Jewish refugees.[9] The quest for the establishment of a Jewish homeland in Palestine as the only solution to worldwide anti-Semitism increased.[10] Through the work of Hecht Neighborhood House, the Associated Jewish Philanthropies, the American Jewish Congress, and the *Jewish Advocate*, Boston's Jews attempted to deal with their ethnic identity in constructive ways.[11]

In praising the contributions made by Jewish war veterans, the *Jewish Advocate* illustrated the significance of a Jewish American identity. "Proud of their Americanism, they have in no way sought to diminish or minimize their Jewish pride, conscious that to do so would be a scorn of the freedom afforded by democracy."[12] Perhaps the experience of the diaspora served to heighten communal bonds during periods of acute international crisis. Perhaps, too, a historic Jewish awareness of the Holocaust reaffirmed the primacy of the ethnic group. "We dare not let ourselves become indifferent to pain and grief," the *Jewish Advocate* vowed.[13] "It may hurt, constantly to be conscious of the brutalities suffered by our brethren, but better the hurt, better the stab of heartache, than the inhuman, cold spirit anesthetized against appreciation of human misery and suffering and want."[14] In their vigorous opposition to anti-Semitism, the subversive activities of the Nazi and Italian consulates in Boston, and the flourishing of the Christian Front, Boston's Jews frequently clashed with Irish and Italians.[15] But these manifestations of ethnic conflict did not resemble the hysterical Irish antisubversive witch-hunts or the frenzied Italian profascist street demonstrations. Rather, the strong institutional structure of Boston's Jewish community prevented the outbursts of hostilities that ignited South Boston and the North End. On occasion, Jews lashed out at a Christian world that allowed Hitler to flourish: "It did not have to happen if the forces of Christianity throughout the world had risen at the first persecution of Jews in Hitler's Reich."[16] Similiarly, the *Advocate* looked with dread upon the isolationist utterances of Charles A. Lindbergh. "It is fair to say that anti-Semitism has assumed a 'respectability' which it never had before even in the days of the Ku Klux Klan."[17] Overall, Boston's Jewish community strove to assert democratic values in a world gone mad with hate and violence.

The impact of the international system reinforced a commitment to liberal social and political ideals. The realization that anti-Semitism in the United States was merely an extension of international violence and hate caused Boston's Jewish community to redouble their efforts on behalf of democracy. "The anti-Semitic campaign conducted in this country on a tremendous scale forbodes the destruction of American institutions and, eventually, the doom of man."[18] This outlook contrasted with the obstructionist cast of Irish and Italian isolationism, Anglophobia, and anticommunism. In this atmosphere the omnipresent specter of human suffering, particularly that induced by anti-Semitism, stirred Boston's Jews deeply. Louis Kirstein, a leader of stature and influence, summed up the sense of mission confronting Boston's Jews in the face of the Nazi Holocaust. "News about the distress of some people is particularly mortifying—many of them have been great benefactors of mankind and are now suffering because mad lust for power happens to be in the saddle in Germany to which they brought so much glory and so much gain," Kirstein declared. "And so, a contribution on their behalf is not an act of charity to distinguished people in distress but an act of duty, of response to a striking symbol of distinguished service, to truth-seeking, and therefore, to humanity."[19]

The chaos of the international system tended to reaffirm the primacy of democratic institutions throughout the world. "When the religious groups are aloof and unresponsive to the persecution of other groups totalitarianism may result as in Germany."[20] At Hecht House the crucial role played by democratic institutions was a constant theme. The staff of social workers understood well the impact that the war and anti-Semitism had on Jewish youth. As the executive director recalled:

> Throughout these years there was another theme. Our boys and girls were Jews. Many of them knew little about their Jewish background and became confused and disturbed because of growing anti-Semitism. We tried to make them comfortable and happy as Jews; we tried to make them understand that Judaism has a rich background, that it has always stood for the brotherhood of man, and that, today, Judaism has a rightful place in a democratic state.

Therefore, our job is basically the same as it has been throughout
the last decade—to help young Jewish people to understand democracy and to prepare them to take their place in our democratic state.
War only heightens this emphasis. Our members know the terrors of
another way of life—fascism, and are beginning to appreciate the
values of democracy.[21]

Indeed, by 1941, 1942, and 1943, Boston's Jewish community served
as the forefront of liberalism in Boston. By 1944 Jewish wards were
the most steadfast supporters of the Roosevelt administration. In
fact, F.D.R.'s strength in Jewish neighborhoods increased by over
20 percent while it decreased by 18 percent in South Boston and 24
percent in the North End and East Boston. The enormous pluralities
that Roosevelt received reflected Jewish gratitude for more than a
decade of enlightened social and economic leadership during peace
and war.[22]

In liberal social welfare matters Boston's Jews led every other
ethnic group in Boston. In its call for an investigation of Nazi and
fascist groups in the United States, the *Advocate* warned against
permitting the investigation "to degenerate into an indiscriminate
alien-baiting campaign."[23] Similarly, the *Advocate* condemned
discrimination against Italian Americans because of the abuses of
Mussolini's regime.[24] As the tempo of anti-Semitic activities in
Boston increased, the *Advocate* cautioned against blaming American Catholics for the activities of the Christian Front and Coughlinites.[25] Even during the worst onslaughts of anti-Semitism in
Boston between 1942 and 1944, the official spokesmen of Jewish
Boston led the fight for the elimination of racial and religious discrimination.[26] By mid-decade, Jews were the most steadfast supporters of the National Association for the Advancement of Colored People and civil rights in Boston.[27]

The chaos of the international system promoted the development
of a secular messianism that was expressed in ethnic solidarity and
political liberalism. When war finally came on December 7, 1942,
the *Advocate* pledged: "Unity based on a common acceptance of
the truth that democracy worth having is worth defending, will
become the keynote of the Jewish adjustment to the emerging
period."[28]

The liberalism and ethnic solidarity characteristic of Jewish leaders in the 1940s was symbolized best in a personal sideline of the Atlantic Charter. Louis Kirstein had given President Roosevelt a gift of three neckties from his department store where Roosevelt's son, John Roosevelt, worked before the war.[29] At the historic meeting off the coast of Newfoundland on August 9, 1941, Franklin D. Roosevelt presented one of the neckties to Prime Minister Churchill. "The gift to the President—and hence, to Churchill—symbolically represented the support and affection which the Jewish community had bestowed upon the Roosevelts during the course of eight years."[30]

The Italians

The imminence of American involvement in World War II placed enormous strains upon Boston's Italian Americans as well. On one hand, the Italians faced the prospects of "fighting against their own *parentala*" with little enthusiasm if not outright dread.[31] On the other hand, the Hub's Italians recognized their allegiance to the United States. The frequently contradictory pulls between the international system and an Italian American ethnic identity illustrated much about a distinctive Italian culture in Boston. Although Boston's Italians unhesitatingly chose to serve the United States in the aftermath of Pearl Harbor, the period from January 1, 1940, to December 7, 1941, documented the impact of the international system on the shaping of an Italian American world view.[32]

The *Gazzetta del Massachusetts* and the *Italian News* continued to support Italy's foreign policies. Thus the Hub's Italian American newspapers, like the Italian American press generally, were ". . . forced to explain away all Axis aggression."[33] Central to this perspective was the argument that the Italian-German Axis was simply an expression of traditional European imperialism. As the *Gazzetta del Massachusetts* explained:

> Let us begin by facing facts frankly and sanely.
> This war in Europe is not a war of high principles and noble ideals on either side.
> It is a conflict of selfish interests and material objectives.
> It is a war between established imperialisms and intended and proposed imperialisms.

It is a war between the haves and have-nots in imperialistic possessions.

It is a war between France and England on the one side and Germany and Italy on the other. . . .

Germany wants to secure now, first her own territorial limits, second, her former possessions, and, third, the right to expand imperial-
ly as England and France have done.

This is what lebensraum—living space—means.

Italy has not lost any possessions, but she has not obtained the
possessions she was promised by treaty when she was induced to
support the Allies in the late war.

Italy has natural aspirations to become an empire like France and
England.

Mussolini has exciting and inciting visions of the glory that was
Greece and the grandeur that was Rome.[34]

Similarly, the *Italian News* minced no words in its outspoken
editorials:

Let John Bull, who stole most of what he has, fight his own war for
the first time in his outrageous career.

The life of one American is to be considered infinitely above John
Bull's greed.

It's their quarrel in Europe, not ours—the claims of British propagandists notwithstanding.

If our country enters the war—heaven forbid—the blood of
American dead and maimed will be upon the hands of Great Britain's
puppets here.[35]

Despite the isolationism and Anglophobia, there were distinct
changes in the outlooks of Boston's Italian press six and one-half
years after the frenzied outpouring of support for the Italian war in
Ethiopia. The painful pull of Italian and American allegiances in
1940-41 tended to limit unqualified expressions of Italian nationalism. Boston's Italians forcefully supported the Italo-Ethiopian
war because it provided them with self-esteem. Italian victories in
Africa made Italy a power of international stature. The Italian-
German Axis contributed little in the way of prestige, however.
Moreover, the prospects of Italian Americans fighting Italians produced only apprehension. Thus when President Roosevelt denounced the Italian invasion of France as a "stab-in-the-back," the

speech caused indignation in the North End and East Boston but not outrage.[36] Undoubtedly such a speech would have caused a furor in Italian neighborhoods six years earlier. Fundamentally, the international system imposed painful strains on Italian American identity in Boston as the complexity of international events revealed in 1940 and 1941.

The Hub's Italian press tried to ignore these explicit contradictions by embracing virulent isolationism and Anglophobia. Time and again the *Italian News* gave front-page coverage to the irrational tirades of Anglophobic Irishmen. The *Italian News* printed with approval Senator Walsh's isolationist rhetoric: "When have the German Government or the German people ever done anything to us as a nation, that should cause us to go to war? When have the Italian Government or the Italian people ever said anything against our Government or our people or usurped any of our resources or committed a single unfriendly act against us?"[37] Similarly, the *News* carried detailed reports of Irish denunciations of the British.[38] "People...who oppose and expose this tide of British falsehoods, are branded either a Fascist or a Communist'. In other words we are either pro-British or anti-American," the *News* observed. "This form of logic is typical of the small minds guiding the future destinies of our country at present. They see the truth but close their eyes, blinded by the shining glitter of British gold—not that they hate Germany or Italy, but because they love prestige, power, and wealth."[39]

But the inherent difficulties of being Italian American as the United States drifted closer to war with the Axis Powers could not be ignored. The choice between Italy and the United States was a difficult one to make. "We are Americans to the core and we too, if necessary, would point a gun and shoot at Italians or anybody else if Uncle Sam deems it necessary," the *News* declared. "But we would do it in the knowledge that we are killing the thing we loved. Because we want the whole world to know that we love Italy and that our affection is more than skin deep."[40] City Councilor Joseph Russo expressed this outlook as well. Russo rose in the city council to speak against a motion by Councilor Gottlieb congratulating the Department of State for closing Nazi and Italian consulates in the United States. "Mr. President, I feel that the action of the United

States Government in closing particularly the Italian consulates does not cast reflection as far as any Americans of Italian origin are concerned here in America." As Russo argued:

> The people of Italian extraction in America have demonstrated their loyalty to America in the past, have demonstrated their loyalty to America at the present, and I am fully confident that they will demonstrate their loyalty in the future. But I do state, Mr. President, as was expressed in the resolution that I put forth sometime ago, that I do believe and firmly believe that this is not our war.[41]

The Japanese attack on Pearl Harbor resolved the dilemma confronting the Italian American residents of the North End and East Boston. Italian Americans overwhelmingly chose to serve the United States. The *Gazzetta del Massachusetts* proclaimed the "united American determination to win the war."[42] "The war has finally come to us—and for us the choice is simple," the *News* stated. "In this hour of crisis a united America will follow its ancient tradition. And as once again we take up arms to preserve our country, this time against a treacherous Japan, we mutually pledge to each other our Lives, our Fortunes, and our Sacred Honor."[43]

Thus, the impact of the international system resolved the dilemma confronting Italian Americans in Boston as in the Little Italys throughout the United States. Allegiance to the United States and active participation in the American war effort did not involve the "sacrifice" of traditional loyalty for Italy.[44] Both Italian Americans and non-Italian Americans distinguished between the people of Italy and Mussolini's aggressive aspirations. Ironically, Italy as a primary symbol of Italian American ethnic attachments remained unscathed.[45] Italian American support for U.S. objectives in the war proved their loyalty and patriotism to the United States. But it also included a love for the fatherland independent of Mussolini. Indeed, Italian American support for the American war effort demonstrated the resilience of both an Italian and American identity. It also illustrated its complexity.

The Irish

Irish reactions to the coming of World War II, at least in South Boston, were more difficult to assess than either Jewish or Italian perspectives. The strains of a difficult ethnic past and an uncertain future were manifest in Irish institutions. The Boston Irish approached American involvement in World War II with great reluctance. Instead of viewing the activities of Nazi Germany as inimical to American democracy and world peace, the Boston Irish chose to indulge their parochial perspectives by ignoring and distorting the inevitability of world war. Irish Boston's central political and religious institutions reinforced these ethnic outlooks. Just as the Boston Irish would endorse the flowering of anti-Semitism in 1942, 1943, and 1944 by their silence and inaction, communal leaders tended to reduce the approaching war in Europe to ridiculous platitudes and sometimes appalling oversimplifications. Indeed, Irish reactions to the coming of World War II revealed profoundly important interactions between the international system and life in Boston that often resulted in Irish-Jewish ethnic conflict between 1942 and 1944.

Isolationism, anticommunism, and still acute Anglophobia characterized the principal dimensions of the Irish reaction to the war in Europe. These outlooks were loaded with ethnic overtones, thus providing them with extraordinary emotional power. In many respects, the Boston Irish justified their isolationism, anticommunism, and Anglophobia on the kind of flimsy emotional rhetoric that Father Coughlin and other revisionists used to explain the causes of World War I. Two of the foremost leaders of Irish Boston vigorously endorsed American isolationism: Massachusetts' senior Senator David I. Walsh and William Cardinal O'Connell. Each man illustrated the role that Irish identity played during a period of heightening international tensions and accelerating domestic insecurity. Both Walsh and O'Connell epitomized the failure of effective and positive leadership in the Irish community as a whole.

As the likelihood of American military participation in World War II approached, Senator Walsh seemed almost panic stricken. Increasingly, Walsh found himself in the company of America's foremost isolationists—Charles A. Lindbergh and Senators Millard E. Tydings, Joel B. Clark, Rush D. Holt, and Dennis Chavez. Walsh railed at the thought of the approaching American involvement in Europe.[46] He warned the American people of the dire consequences of American participation in World War II. "There will be a radical psychology developed in this country that will be very, very dangerous in the future," Walsh predicted.[47] As the chairman of the powerful Naval Affairs Committee, Walsh's stand on isolationism had more than passing national significance. In June 1940, Walsh threatened to resign from the Senate rather than "vote to put the United States in war."[48] Walsh decried the administration's foreign policy "as too risky, too dangerous," adding that the United States should be willing to "live in the same world with a tyrant—we have been doing it for 150 years."[49]

One of the critical showdowns between President Roosevelt and his isolationist opponents came during the first week of August 1941, when the administration pressed for the extension of the Selective Service Act. Walsh vigorously opposed the extension charging that F.D.R.'s policy was designed "to lead us day by day into war."[50] The Senate passed the Extension Bill by a vote of 45 to 30, but in the House a single vote resulted in its passage.[51]

The almost frantic apprehensions with which Senator Walsh viewed American involvement in Europe were not without irony. David I. Walsh began his political career thirty years earlier with a liberalism that appealed to all of Massachusetts' ethnic groups. During the years of seething nativism in the 1920s—the Americanization movement, the Ku Klux Klan, and the Sacco and Vanzetti trial—the young Irish Democrat lashed out at bigotry and nativism in all its manifestations.[52] By the summer of 1941, however, Senator Walsh frantically looked for reasons to explain American involvement with Britain. Walsh found these explanations in an increasingly defensive and strident ethnic outlook. For example, Walsh lashed out at the "demands" of "propagandists and pressure groups who are thinking of every part of the world except the United States."[53] Certainly these "propagandists and pressure groups" included the standard list—Anglophiles, big businessmen, and munitions' manufacturers. The fact that Walsh resorted to such flimsy "conspiracy theses" so much in vogue in the 1920s and 1930s represented the paucity of his social and political thought in the 1940s. The vague references to "propagandists and pressure groups" so akin to Coughlin's rhetoric seemed to bring David I. Walsh's closing political career full circle—from political liberalism to illiberal politics. Senator Walsh reflected as well as molded an

Irish Catholic reaction to the international system. Walsh's increasingly strident and rancorous outbursts contributed to the absence of constructive outlooks in Irish Boston, to be sure. Senator Walsh best expressed the alienation and bitter frustrations of this perspective in his reaction to the Atlantic Charter. In the face of the pledge by Franklin D. Roosevelt and Winston S. Churchill to defeat Nazi aggression, guarantee fundamental human freedoms, and build a lasting and just world order, David I. Walsh railed at the presumptuousness of F.D.R.'s actions. Walsh characterized the historic meeting at sea as a commitment "that goes far beyond the Constitutional powers of the President and one that no other President in our history ever presumed to assume."⁵⁴ Blinded by strident isolationism and Irish rancor to the fundamental threats posed by Nazi Germany, Senator Walsh decried the decline of American civilization resulting from entangling European alliances. "The worst of the matter is that the American people have been afforded no opportunity to pass judgement," Walsh declared. "Congress and the Constitutional concepts of representative government have been brushed aside, and the President alone, and on his own initiative, has undertaken to pledge our government, our nation, and the lives of 130,000,000 persons and their descendants for generations to come."⁵⁵

The letters that the Massachusetts congressional delegation received from the Boston Irish document strong currents of isolationism, Anglophobia, and anticommunism as well. A heightened sense of Irish bitterness and frustration infused these perspectives. As one member of Boston's Irish community wrote:

> Let J. Bull take his beating like a man. Hitler got one ahead of them, therefore, America has to lose her blood and money to save the English rats. England has been a savage oppressor. Does she forget it? . . . The American citizens demand a "No Vote," so as not to let any one or a pampered few or groups to sell us out to a slaughter house for nothing or no come back.
>
> Who then will enjoy the American spoils? Some more dirty J. Bull refugees. . . .
>
> We parents demand no more wars for foreigners. If any body

tackled us, we women can, and would fight gallantly home here on our own soil. No foreigners walking or riding about would be safe . . . .

Let the New Dealer and his pets, and yes henchman be put on the front firinglines. Let Ickes, Wallace, Knox, Stimson, Hull, Morgenthau and others get ready themselves for first line shooting as we Americans will demand and insist upon it . . . .

We Americans will be so enraged by this gang that our nerves and patience will be so exhausted that dangerous methods will prevail.[56]

A less frenzied letter pleaded: "Do not follow the foolish, and warlike foreign policy of the President and the other War Mongers. We do not want to send our boys into a foreign war. I hope there are enough real Americans in the House to defeat this neutrality change. . . . When this English propaganda cools off there will be a terrible reaction against the War Mongers. The President has carried his private war too far."[57]

Another member of Boston's Irish community pleaded: "Show your love for your country by thinking of America first—the way the English love their country to the extent of thinking of England first regardless of anybody else!"[58] Attorney Walter T. Burke probably expressed the fundamental currents of opinion in Irish Boston when he stated: "The great rank and file of the people are thoroughly disgusted with the dishonest means that are being taken to plunge us into the disaster of war without regard for the provisions of the Constitution." Burke concluded, "If those who seek to drag us into war were real Americans they would insist that our Constitution be observed and that if we are to enter into war it should only be after a declaration by the Congress."[59]

Emphasis on "we-they" real Americans (the Irish) vs. Anglophiles, liberals, foreigners, war mongers, and New Dealers characterized each of these letters. The isolation and frustration of the Boston Irish were illustrated by these statements. Like their periodic antisubversive binges of the 1930's, the force of the international system in the 1940s stimulated a hostile vision of the world surrounding South Boston, Dorchester, and Roxbury. These outbursts of nativism and xenophobia, like the resurgence of anti-

Semitism between 1942 and 1944, document the interactions between the international system and the historical setting of ethnicity in Irish neighborhoods. Political institutions certainly contributed to a defensive climate of opinion. However, political
leaders like David I. Walsh hardly defined the full ramifications of
Irish hostility. The leadership of Boston's Catholic church was a
significant variable.

William Cardinal O'Connell was no less outspoken in his apprehensions about American involvement in World War II than David
I. Walsh. In the cardinal's pronouncements, in the editorial pages
of the *Boston Pilot*, and through the clergy of the archdiocese,
O'Connell significantly contributed to the shaping of opinion in
Boston's Irish enclaves. During a period when Irish Catholics turned
to the church for spiritual consolation, Boston's Catholic hierarchy
offered graphic if simplistic descriptions of current international
politics.

Despite his often combative predispositions in the running of the
archdiocese, O'Connell embraced a decidedly pacific stance on
matters of world peace. The preservation of "peace" and American
innocence were frequent themes that his eminence invoked. On his
birthday, December 7, 1940, the cardinal issued a typical command
to his flock "to beseech God's prudent direction to the leaders of
our beloved country so that the nation's peace will continue." But
the cardinal's desire for peace assumed a purely spiritual form. In
spite of the power of the Nazi war machine, O'Connell preferred to
place the ultimate solution to Nazi aggression in the hands of God.
Such an outcome precluded active American participation in the
European conflagration. "Let us all unite in beseeching the Queen
of Peace to intercede with her Divine Son that He may send His
peace to the distracted world," O'Connell prayed, "and His wise
counsel and prudent direction to the leaders of our beloved country
that we may continue in that peace which is one of heaven's
choicest gifts."[60]

The power of prayer may have given the aging prelate spiritual
consolation, but on less introspective occasions Cardinal O'Connell took a back seat to no one in articulating a militant isolationism. O'Connell believed the United States should keep out of

the war and work for peace. Like Senator Walsh and Father Coughlin, the cardinal railed against "propagandists for war" at home.[61] The cardinal's militance sharply contrasted with his more spiritually inclined moods. However, whether he was invoking the power of prayer or the power of political organization, a distinctive Irish outlook pervaded O'Connell's influential leadership. For example, he skillfully paid lip service to the quest for world peace—a peace clearly impossible without direct American participation. "Not only should we keep out of war for America and Americans but we might well be turning our thoughts toward a speedy and permanent peace among the nations...." the cardinal declared. "Notwithstanding the too prevalent propaganda from all sides, the hope and prayer of the American people today is that we shall be spared the horrors of war. They have taken for granted what the authorities at Washington meant when they promised to keep us out of war."[62]

If O'Connell reflected a widespread revulsion against the specter of war generally, he could also get down to concrete issues without the slightest difficulty. Like United States participation in World War I, American entrance in the war in Europe rested on the manipulation of skillful propagandists. In invoking this popular thesis, O'Connell pandered to fundamental ethnic fears and prejudices. "It is hard for me to understand why some of the propagandists are allowed to cry down the normal wish of the American people for peace. What is their purpose? They cannot be *real Americans*, because *real Americans* think of their own country first," his eminence concluded. "There are *certain expatriates*, I think you know whom I mean—who are raising their voices in *loud accents* with the preposterous proposition that America sink her individuality and become a sort of tail-end of a foreign empire. If this is not an example of exalted hysteria, I don't know what it could be."[63] For Cardinal O'Connell and the Boston Irish, references to "propagandists," "certain expatriates," and "loud accents" implied the collusion of Anglophiles, liberals, and Jews. In the political, cultural, and psychological setting of Irish Boston, the cardinal's pointed references had explosive ethnic overtones. This explicit lack of vision pervaded other communal institutions as well. For example, members of the St. Brendan Society lobbied vigorously to prevent any changes in American neutrality. As they explained to the Massachusetts congressional delegation:

> The St. Brendan Society, an organization composed of men and women, fathers and mothers and citizens of your district, voted unanimously at a recent meeting to ask your support against any further changes in our present neutrality law.
>
> We do not presume that you would give any other aim your support, but we feel that at this time, when the most intelligent minds we have are confused, there is a chance for hasty action by Congress upon measures regarding our neutrality act. Amidst the "pressure" in Washington from all sides and bombarded with every angle and argument, it is a wonder that Congress has been able to keep us from the "European War."
>
> We feel that because of the Neutrality Act we have saved that precious mystery we call "Life." We ask God in His Goodness to help you solve this problem in the best way for America, and we respectfully suggest you continue to seek His help for a clearer understanding of how best to protect this wonderful nation and millions of lives.[64]

The *Boston Pilot* also played a central role in advancing staunchly isolationist perspectives. Like David I. Walsh and Cardinal O'Connell, the influential editors of the *Pilot* were preoccupied by the specter of global war. In its editorials, the interpretation of news, and the molding of public opinion, the *Pilot* further reinforced a perspective that in turn reinforced differences between Irish and Jews. Isolationism, Anglophobia, and anticommunism were issues around which Irish ethnic animosities emerged.

The explicit isolationist, Anglophobic, and anticommunist threads in the *Pilot's* editorial pages tended to merge together. However, a distinctive Irish outlook crystalized in the 1940s as it had in the 1930s. Consequently, isolationism, Anglophobia, and anticommunism were colored by ethnic overtones. Central to this dynamic was the long-standing Irish apprehension of Godless communism that reinforced a contempt for liberal America. The *Pilot* lashed out at the double standard implied in liberal support for communism and opposition to fascism. With prospects of Anglo-Soviet-American military cooperation rising, the *Pilot* took the of-

fensive. An editor asked rather pointedly "if the allies will only sub-
due Germany and not Russia?"[65] The extermination of Jews and the
persecution of Catholics throughout German-occupied territory
notwithstanding, the *Pilot* continued its anti-Soviet tirades. "Probably the most *barren* spot on earth, from a spiritual point of view,
is *Russia.* Here war against God never relents.... Almost as bad is
Germany.... Most irritating is the case of Mexico. Here we have
religious peace endangered where an enlightened attitude by our
government would compel respect for all rights."[66] Once again the
Pilot raised the rancorous issue of liberal insensitivities to Irish
Catholic interests. The perceived social inferiority of Boston's Irish
Catholics must have influenced this perspective. The *Pilot* never
tired of pointing to the hypocrisy of self-righteous American
liberals. "But since the choice is not between communal ownership
and capitalism but between God and anti-God, they cannot kill a
kindly feeling for Communism. We shall hear from them again. We
shall find their voices raised in championship of any liberal pro-
posal aimed to promote human indulgence at the expense of
God."[67]

The realization of German persecution of Jews and Catholics
raised fundamental ethical problems, however. On occasion, the
Pilot lashed out at Nazism and communism in a kind of "plague on
both your houses" condemnation. The *Pilot* called upon Americans
not to ally themselves with either "Godless camp."[68] Fundamentally, it was an Irish Catholic opposition to communism that
determined the *Pilot's* editorial pronouncement in the early 1940s.
This ghettoized perspective pitted the faithful stalwart Boston Irish
against far less patriotic New Dealers, atheists, liberals, and Jews.
As the war became imminent, the *Pilot* intensified its rhetoric.

> Communists are consistent everywhere. Their tactics alter with
> circumstances.... But it remains unalterably true that Communism
> is an enemy of God.
>   And Communism is an enemy of democracy. How much more
> evidence shall we require before we accept this fact that the authen-
> tic Communist can never be a trustworthy ally of any democratic na-
> tion? We have all the proof reasonable minds should ask. And still,
> there are those who insist on applying a *variable standard of morals*
> to Germany and Russia. The wrong things of Nazism they condemn

with a ringing and bitter emphasis. Nazism, they say, must be destroyed as evil in essence. But these amateur moralists show an odd tolerance for the crimes of Communism. They do not approve. But they disapprove mildly. They are glib with extenuations. They say it is impossible to live in the same world with Nazism. But they are cheerfully willing to trade with Communists, exchange pleasant greetings with them, and even— if the issue should be presented—to fight by their side in war to "preserve democracy."[69]

In this political, socioeconomic, and cultural setting ethnic conflict was almost inevitable. If the *Pilot* reserved the full fury of its invective for communists and fellow travelers, it did not underplay its Anglophobia and isolationism either. In their defense of Ireland's neutrality, the editors of the *Pilot* revealed an equally strident outlook. Ethnic issues were of more than passing concern. The Boston Irish were somewhat perplexed by the moral and ethical problems involved in the question of Irish neutrality. Senator Walsh expressed his fondest hopes that Ireland would remain neutral throughout the course of World War II.[70] Despite their vehement protests to the contrary, the editors of the *Pilot* were embarrassed by Ireland's refusal to fight Nazi Germany. The involved arguments and contrived rationalizations illustrated a profound defensiveness. The question that Eire's neutrality posed went right to the heart of an Irish perspective. "The most consistent logic England can bring to bear upon the present situation cannot alter or remove Ireland's right to remain neutral," the *Boston Pilot* argued. Apparently, English sins of the past far outweighed Ireland's responsibility to oppose German aggression. "That question must be decided by the people of Eire. Irishmen have always defended their native soil. They propose to do so in the present critical times. No one can question their right, their courage, their reasonableness, if they now refuse to become part of a war effort conducted by an alien country."[71]

On less strident occasions, the *Pilot* reminded its readers that Ireland was one of the few remaining republics in the world. Therefore, Ireland could not afford to have the war disrupt the evolution of its democratic processes.[72] Such a perspective illustrated the defensiveness that characterized Irish elites in Boston. Doubts occasionally surfaced, however. The editors of the *Pilot* conceded: "The position of this small nation is very difficult, the factors influencing Irish decisions are so complex that no satisfactory policy is possible. Whatever attitude is adopted will certainly suffer criticism."[73]

Bitterness, skepticism, and frustration lingered throughout the late fall of 1941. The contradictions implicit in isolationism, Irish neutrality, Anglophobia, and opposition to communism in the face of Nazi tyranny placed enormous strains on an Irish perspective. Even in the traumatic days following Pearl Harbor, the *Pilot* was strangely subdued. War finally had come to the United States. Perhaps the editors of the *Pilot* sensed that with the coming of World War II a new unchartered course was about to begin. "The strategists will explain how this condition came about. In their own fashion they will elaborate the reasons why this war must be fought to a finish. They will demonstrate to their own complete satisfaction and possibly ours—that the enemy must be so completely beaten that we, whose purposes are pure beyond any breath of suspicion, may dictate the peace," the *Pilot* sardonically stated. "But surely we may be pardoned for remembering that war means hatreds blown to unreasoning flame. War signifies death for the flower of our youth. It means heart-break at home. Not for nothing have we personified war as Mars—the god whose symbols were the wolf, the woodpecker and the lance."[74]

The future was indeed uncertain. Tens of thousands of Boston Irishmen would fight in World War II. Many thousands would not return home. But the actions of other less gallant individuals would prevail in South Boston, Dorchester, and Roxbury. The resurgence of anti-Semitism in the 1940s confirmed the destructiveness of certain paranoid segments of Irish Boston. The violence of the world war perhaps stimulated increasing patterns of violence in these neighborhoods. Moreover, the war drained many thousands of young men and women from Irish neighborhoods. Perhaps those that remained were among the most marginal and destructive elements of the society. In this context, the structural setting of ethnicity in Boston—political institutions, socioeconomic variables, cultural and psychological world views—merged with the force of the international environment bringing about repeated manifestations of ethnic conflict in 1942, 1943, and 1944.

THE RESURGENCE OF ANTI-SEMITISM

The precise dynamics of Irish anti-Semitism between 1942 and 1944 have been obscured by the passage of time, guilt, shame, and the suppression of evidence.[75] As the American people mobilized to combat German and Japanese aggression, anti-Semitism became *prima facie* evidence of disloyalty. The United States Department of Justice finally suppressed the publication of Father Coughlin's newspaper *Social Justice* in 1942 because of its seditious character. Consequently, the attractiveness of anti-Semitism as a respectable ideological perspective rapidly diminished for the majority of Americans at least on an overt level. In the tense years of the 1940s, Father Coughlin's message of hate and violence crystallized in a number of Irish enclaves in the United States: New York, Philadelphia, and Boston. Thus the fairly muted anti-Semitic hostilities of the 1930s gave way to the outbreak of explicit anti-Semitism of frightening intensity and surprising dimensions in several Irish sections.

The existence of Coughlin's profascist organization, the Christian Front, provided the ideological and institutional bases that facilitated the growth of organized anti-Semitic activities. Coughlin sponsored the formation of the Christian Front in 1938 at the time when his anti-Semitism and profascism reached unprecedented heights. The Christian Front was composed of a number of rifle clubs and "quasi-military squads of young men" strikingly similar to German "storm troopers."[76] Father Coughlin pointed out in *Social Justice* that, "It is gratifying to learn that so many people are interested in making arrangements for the establishment of platoons 'against the day' when they will be needed. The day is not far distant in the future."[77] In 1939 the Christian Front launched an intensive wave of anti-Semitic activities in New York City.[78] Irish gangs attacked Jews in Brooklyn and Queens, synagogues were desecrated, and Jewish stores boycotted.[79] Father Coughlin commanded his audience to "Buy Christian for Christmas" while he "pleaded" with Jews not to take Christmas away from Christians.[80]

The Federal Bureau of Investigation arrested seventeen members of the Christian Front in New York on January 13, 1940. The FBI seized a number of rifles, clubs, and homemade bombs when it raided the Christian Front meeting. The Department of Justice prosecuted the seventeen members of the Christian Front on the basis of "conspiring to overthrow the government of the United States by force." The defendants were acquitted on June 24, 1940.[81]

The Christian Front continued its activities in New York and Boston during the 1940s. The front secured a foothold in South Boston and Roxbury during the latter years of the 1930s. The church, political leaders, and other Irish institutions directly contributed to an atmosphere in which anti-Semitism would take hold because of the absence of constructive communal leadership. The traditional ghettoization of South Boston reinforced the attractiveness of anti-Semitic activities. From an ecclesiastical perspective, there is little doubt that Cardinal O'Connell held Father Coughlin and the Christian Front in contempt. Moreover, O'Connell's personal relations with members of Boston's Jewish community were cordial.[82] Despite the cardinal's sincere and honest abhorrence of racism and anti-Semitism, the course of international events often dictated philosophical, ideological, and political stands that contradicted his personal support for religious tolerance. Thus issues such as communism, isolationism, and Anglophobia tended to obscure concern for anti-Semitism in Boston. O'Connell, for example, adopted a hands-off policy regarding the activities of the Christian Front in Boston. His spokesmen could even defend the front on occasion. When the seventeen members of the front were tried for sedition in New York by the U.S. Department of Justice, the Rev. Michael J. Ahern, S. J. published a revealing defense of the Christian Front in the *Boston Post*. "I am inclined to agree with the verdict of 'America' that the real culprits were not the 17 men arrested but the instigators of their arrest," Ahern declared. "Many seem to have forgotten that before the law a man is innocent until he is proved guilty. The issues of the Christian Front and anti-Semitism so prominent in the scarehead headlines were already quashed before the end of the trial in June."[83]

Such Irish defensiveness often dictated the position that the church assumed on important issues. This lack of constructive leadership in the face of heightening anti-Semitic activities in part contributed to the resurgence of anti-Semitism in the 1940s.

Coughlinites noticeably increased their activities in Boston in 1941 and 1942. Francis P. Moran served as the New England leader of the Christian Front. Under his leadership, Boston became the focal point for the front's New England activities. Moran launched Boston's anti-Semitic campaign on June 3, 1941, with the screening of the gruesome Nazi propaganda film *Sieg in Westen* (*Victory in the West*). Moran showed *Sieg in Westen* at Hibernian Hall in Roxbury where the sessions were "jammed with frenzied pro-Fascism, hate-the-Jew sermons, and inflammatory speech making."[84] The film depicted the brutal Nazi invasion of Poland and was followed by Moran's tirades. Moran told his audiences that the film represented Nazi invincibility and how futile it would be to oppose Germany. Moran branded Winston Churchill a swine and accused Franklin D. Roosevelt of planning to establish a personal dictatorship in the United States. His anti-Semitic references were unmistakable. Moran's rhetoric was confused but he got his points across. He repeatedly told his audiences that F.D.R. placed fifteen hundred anti-Christians in Washington jobs.[85] Several other groups assisted the Christian Front in spreading the radio priest's doctrines of hate and violence. The Social Justice Guild of Boston and the American Mothers Neutrality League of Boston embraced a strident isolationism as well. In addition, a number of members of New York's Christian Front regularly visited Boston—Father Edward Lodge Curran, John Henninghan, Jr., George P. Grunning, Jr., and J. P. Moriarity.[86]

Without a doubt, the institutional setting of Boston's Irish community helped to foster, if only through neglect, an atmosphere in which Coughlinite groups thrived on bitterness and frustrations. Explicit anti-Semitism attempted to compensate for many ills of the Irish ghetto—alcoholism, low rates of socioeconomic mobility, and a sense of defeatism and failure.[87] This mood facilitated the frightening outbursts of anti-Semitic activities in 1942 and 1943.

The scheduled appearance of the Coughlin disciple, Father Edward Lodge Curran, as the principal speaker at South Boston's Evacuation Day Program on March 16, 1942, brought the specter of Irish support for Coughlinism to a head in the Hub. Father Curran was editor of the largest Catholic weekly in the United States, the *Brooklyn Tablet*, and in later years became a domestic prelate. The ensuing controversy exacerbated already strained relations between Irish and Jews and Irish and Yankees. Moreover, the conflict served as a prelude to the most blatant cases of anti-Semitism in 1943.

Evacuation Day (referred to as Patriot's Day in Boston) commemorated the evacuation of all British forces from Boston in 1776. Coincidentally, Evacuation Day fell on the feast of St. Patrick, March 17, a day of some significance in the life of South Boston. Traditional Evacuation Day oratory hailed the Irish contribution to Boston and the United States. In the tense years of the 1940s, Father Curran's appearance at the Evacuation Day ceremonies had more than passing symbolic value. Irish denizens of South Boston turned a celebration of historical significance for all Bostonians into a blatant protest over real and imagined ethnic grievances. Barely four months after the devastating Japanese attack on the American fleet at Pearl Harbor, the Irish of South Boston invited one of the most outspoken isolationists, Coughlinites, and anti-Semites in America to reconsecrate the American birth of freedom.

Boston's leading politicians ducked the controversy en masse. Mayor Maurice J. Tobin delayed returning to Boston from a vacation in Florida. Governor Leverett Saltonstall announced that he could not accept an invitation to speak but his office stressed that the decision was made before the controversy occurred.[88] Cardinal O'Connell, an important political force in his own right, gave official sanction to Father Curran's appearance, pointing out that it was a matter of courtesy.[89]

There were signs of hope, however. For the first time Boston's major newspapers openly acknowledged the existence of the Christian Front in several Irish sections of the city. "Heretofore," the New York daily *P.M.* observed, "the Front was a strictly taboo subject."[90] Moreover, this was the first time that some members of Boston's Irish community mobilized to denounce the Coughlinite assault on American values and ideals. Frances Sweeney, Grace Lonergan, Dr. H. O'Neil Hencken, and other liberal Irish Catholics formed the American-Irish Defense Association opposing all forms of fascism and anti-Semitism in Boston.[91] Frances Sweeney, secretary of the Defense Association, issued a statement protesting Father Curran's appearance in South Boston. Sweeney pointed out: "The Rev. Edward Lodge Curran, a forceful speaker, a brilliant writer, is the eastern representative, mouthpiece and echo of Rev. Charles E. Coughlin of Detroit. He has spoken and written for Charles E. Coughlin. Charles E. Coughlin is the national leader, the symbol of the Christian Front movement."[92]

As the day of Edward Lodge Curran's address approached, tensions gripped the city. The ensuing controversy placed renewed emphasis on ethnic differences. The Jewish-dominated Executive Committee of the Massachusetts CIO called upon all public officials "to refrain from appearing on the same platform with Fr. Curran."[93] The prospect of Curran's appearance in Boston enraged the Hub's Brahmin-Yankee communities. Donald G. Lothrop, pastor of the Community church, telegraphed Mayor Tobin in Florida, asking him "to use any power he possesses to halt Rev. Fr. Curran's address." Dr. Lothrop called upon the mayor to "...wire your personal views as to propriety of city sanction of an associate of purveyors of Nazi, Fascist and anti-Semitic propaganda as speaker at the pre-Evacuation Day patriotic exercises. Do you approve or do you disapprove? All Boston awaits your answer."[94]

Members of Boston's liberal Jewish and Yankee communities emphatically made known their views. Professor Frederick L. Schuman of Williams College minced no words when he addressed the Ford Hall Forum on March 16. Schuman denounced Edward Lodge Curran as a "Fascist demagogue," and a "disgrace to the Catholic Church." Professor Schuman described Father Curran as "anti-British, anti-Russian, and anti-Semitic, a disciple of Fr. Coughlin who has done Goebbel's work in this country far better than Goebbel's paid agents." Schuman concluded by stating that "Fr. Curran's appearance on a city program should be an object lesson to Bostonians...on 'why we're losing the war.'"[95]

Despite the furor raging over Curran's scheduled address, the Irish-dominated South Boston Evacuation Day Committee reacted with predictable intransigence. Boston City Councilor Joseph M. Scannel of South Boston, the chairman of the Evacuation Day Committee, dismissed the objections of non-Irish Boston. Scannel noted that the committee was "well qualified" and he was satisfied with the selection of Father Curran. The city council as a whole agreed, noting that "Fr. Curran possesses a Christian and patriotic attitude of respect for the sincere beliefs of all men. He has constantly decried bigotry in any form and yesterday reiterated his belief that to hate any man or women is vile and un-American."[96]

The reservations of non-Irish Boston to Father Curran's speech notwithstanding (and perhaps because of them), South Boston witnessed the largest turnout in the history of its Evacuation Day program. In a remarkable display of communal solidarity, two thousand people filled South Boston High School Auditorium in a matter of minutes. Over a thousand more spilled over into the gymnasium where loud speakers were set up to carry Curran's speech. Unlike the boycott of Boston's major political leaders, South Boston's political community attended en masse: President of the South Boston Citizens' Association William Flannegan, Boston School Committeeman Patrick J. Foley, Boston Welfare Commissioner William O. O'Hare, Acting Mayor and Ward 7 Councilor (South Boston) Thomas E. Linnehan, and State Representative John E. Powers.[97]

Tensions were in the air, however. The organizers of the Evacuation Day program were not in a benevolent mood. When Frances Sweeney was discovered sitting at the press table, William B. Gallagher, chairman of the Evacuation Day Committee, ordered her removed from the hall. Two men then confronted Sweeney demanding that she leave the auditorium. As the argument intensified, several hundred women in the front row "rose to their feet and yelled, 'put her out.'" Two men raised Frances Sweeney to her feet, forcibly marching her toward the door. As she was being "escorted" out of the auditorium "scores of women hissed and booed."[98]

When Edward Lodge Curran finally arrived, the mood of the crowd suddenly changed. The people of South Boston gave Father Curran a tumultuous welcome as he was escorted down the main aisle. He was accorded a standing ovation when he mounted the stage. Curran's first words, "I am here," brought the house down. For the most part, Curran's speech dealt with a historical review of Boston's part in the American Revolution. In his concluding remarks, Father Curran addressed himself to the controversy over his appearance in South Boston. In almost predictable rhetoric, Curran lashed out at "internal enemies."[99] He warned his audience of the danger of communists who would deny Americans their fundamental freedom.

> There are internal enemies in the United States of America today. One hundred and sixty-six years ago our internal enemies were those who wished the continuation of foreign rule in America. Today the internal enemies are those who would repeal the Constitution, entrap

the Bill of Rights, destroy freedom of speech and surrender America
to the worldwide atheistic revolution of Communism. To the 20th
century internal enemies in our midst, this is the answer we must give
in memory of those who fought on Dorchester Heights.[100]

It was significant that Edward Lodge Curran chose to focus on
the threat of internal communist-dominated enemies rather than
the threats to American freedom posed by the Axis powers. Father
Curran's rhetoric illustrated the extent to which a significant seg-
ment of the Boston Irish were alienated from the values and ideals
of other Bostonians. The outpouring of support for Father Curran
in South Boston displayed the defensiveness and rancor characteristic of a Boston Irish Catholic world view. From this perspective, it
was a case of the poor struggling Irish victimized once again by the
forces of liberal America (Jews and Brahmin-Yankees). The weight
of Boston's past surely helped to define this world view, but self-
indulgence did not provide a solution to the continuing problem of
Irish adjustment to life in Boston. Indeed, the absence of constructive communal leadership combined with this excessive self-pity
gave the Irish of South Boston, Roxbury, and Dorchester the ra-
tionale for continued withdrawal, isolation, and bitterness. The
shocking revelations of the waves of organized anti-Semitic activities in 1943 lend credence to the profound destructiveness of ethnicity in segments of Boston's Irish community.

ANTI-SEMITISM IN THE STREETS

Bostonians initially greeted the news of renewed waves of anti-
Semitic violence in Dorchester and Mattapan with disbelief. When
Arnold Beichman, an investigative reporter for *P.M.*, asked Governor Saltonstall to comment on reports of anti-Semitic activities in
Boston, the governor shouted him down and had him physically
ejected from his office. Similarly, Boston's Mayor Maurice Tobin
refused to consider the problem seriously.[101] As the waves of violence intensified, the leaders of Boston's Jewish community mobilized against it. First, they confronted Boston Police Commissioner
Joseph T. Timilty with evidence of anti-Semitic acts of violence.
These Jewish leaders pointed to cases involving organized gang attacks on Jews, a rising tide of street violence in Jewish neighbor-

hoods, and attacks on Jewish children in Boston.[102] Timilty promised action and assigned a special detail of thirty-five policemen to patrol Jewish neighborhoods in Dorchester and Mattapan. The violence continued, however. In the face of such ineffective measures, the outcry from Boston's Jewish community increased.

Rabbi Samuel I. Korff of the Congregation Kehilath Jacob in Dorchester appealed to religious leaders of all faiths to fight the accelerating patterns of anti-Semitism in Boston. Rabbi Korff declared: "We can no longer ignore the incidents which have occurred repeatedly in the past few years and discard them as isolated unmotivated hooliganism. These are more than ordinary incidents. The pattern which has been followed during all the attacks indicate definitely that they are of an organized character."[103] A cognizance of the course of European anti-Semitism informed the outlook of Boston's Jewish leaders. The specter of events in Germany was inescapable. "We don't ask for protection as Jews. We ask for the safeguarding of those principles without which this nation cannot exist," Rabbi Korff warned all Bostonians. "History has proven that such incidents cannot be localized. Their purpose is to destroy the foundations of democracy and unless the church and state awaken to the reality and gravity of the situation, the repercussions may be far-reaching in their character."[104]

Despite the reluctance of Boston's political leadership to acknowledge the reality of anti-Semitism in Boston, the Hub's Jewish community pressed its case forward. City Councilor Charles I. Taylor, who represented Jewish neighborhoods at City Hall, substantiated charges of anti-Semitism. Lilian S. Gurvitz, counsel for the New England Division of the American Jewish Congress, provided further proof of extensive anti-Semitic acts. Gurvitz disclosed that the American Jewish Congress had been collecting affidavits from victims of anti-Semitism in Dorchester, Mattapan, and Roxbury for over a year. "In my opinion, however, the many recent assaults have a distinct pattern of anti-Semitic acts," Attorney Gurvitz concluded. "The many affidavits we have taken of incidents during the last two months substantiate the *P.M.* statements."[105] Francis L. Hurwitz, the director of the New England Regional Office of the Anti-Defamation League of B'nai B'rith, attested to the reality of anti-Semitism in Boston. Hurwitz attributed the outbreak of anti-Semitism to the role of enemy propaganda in Boston. "This propaganda has been spreading across the country including Boston and the New England States for some years now and in increasing volume in recent months." Hurwitz called for immediate and forceful action to eliminate the menace of anti-Semitism in Boston.[106]

Pressure for the eradication of anti-Semitism mounted among members of Boston's Yankee community as well. In an outspoken editorial, "Racism in Boston," the *Christian Science Monitor* denounced the existence of anti-Semitism in the Hub. "Boston has been too tolerant of hoodlumism," the *Monitor* charged. "Officials, schools, churches and the public generally in the city and even in the most polite suburbs have suffered a degree of vandalism which would outrage most communities in the 'Wild West.'" In attempting to explain the outbreak of anti-Semitism in Boston, the *Monitor* noted that the "atmosphere of violence brought by the war" may have helped to bring on the attacks. Doubts lingered, however. The *Monitor* conceded that the "pattern of definite anti-Semitism is not so easily explained."[107] "Why, when America as a whole is fighting Hitlerism which rose to power on its persecution of the Jews, should Americans develop a new anti-Semitic feeling so strong it breaks out in the violence of children against children?"[108] Undoubtedly incidents of anti-Semitic violence were more complex than just the impact of intensifying patterns of violence in the international system. "There is, however, plenty of evidence that *some* Americans have become retail outlets for the anti-Semitic propaganda manufactured in Berlin and handed out wholesale by Fascist organizations in the United States."[109] In carefully chosen words, the *Monitor* alluded to the nature of Irish anti-Semitism:

> The poison put out by the Coughlinites and the Christian Front has been seen for what it is by many who once cheered its purveyors at Patriots' Day (Evacuation Day) rallies in South Boston. But *certain elements* of Boston's population have been too tolerant of it. The outrages now coming to light should not be exaggerated. But they certainly cannot be glossed over. They should precipitate vigorous action by officials, civic and church organizations and by all real Americans to neutralize the poison that has been working in

Boston and eradicate the hatreds and prejudices which open channels
for it.[110]

The *Boston Globe* concurred fully. In an editorial, "No Hoodlum
Bigots," the *Globe* demanded an end to anti-Semitism. It declared
that "Boston is in no temper to stand an outbreak of racial and religious intolerance."[111]

In an attempt to defuse the situation, Governor Saltonstall
ordered a statewide investigation by the Massachusetts State Police.
The governor also appointed a special task force to try to stop the
growing anti-Semitic activities in Boston.[112] Continuing revelations
of anti-Semitic incidents heightened tensions in Jewish neighborhoods, however.

Specifically, news of the brutal beating of a seventeen-year-old
Jewish boy by a member of the Boston Police Department enraged
public opinion in Boston generally.[113] On a Saturday night in late
October 1943, two Jewish boys from Dorchester, Jacob Hodas and
Harvey Blaustein, were physically assaulted by a gang of Irish
toughs.[114] The police arrived after both boys had been severely
beaten. The police officers on the scene then dismissed the gang of
hoodlums without making any arrests. When Hodas and Blaustein
protested against such biased action, they were arrested and taken
to Police Station 11 in Dorchester where they were held incom-
municado for a day.[115] Harvey Blaustein was then beaten in a back
room with a length of rubber hose at Police Station 11 by a ranking
member of the Boston Police Department. The officer called Blaustein a "yellow Jew" as he administered the beating.[116] Several days
later Jacob Hodas and Harvey Blaustein were found guilty of par-
ticipating in an "affray" and fined ten dollars.[117] Max Belsky, the
editor of the local neighborhood weekly, the *Dorchester Record*,
probably came closest to reflecting accurately Jewish public opinion
in Roxbury, Dorchester, and Mattapan when he warned: "We are
going to have riots here that will rival Detroit unless something is
done."[118]

Indeed, such blatant anti-Semitism outraged all fair-minded
people of Boston. Some of the most articulate and eloquent denunciations came from liberal Irish Catholics. Joseph F. Dineen, the
popular columnist for the *Globe*, addressed his fellow Bostonians

in a radio broadcast on Wednesday evening, October 27. Recounting the news of the arrests, beatings, and convictions of Jacob Hodas and Harvey Blaustein, Dineen condemned all manifestations of anti-Semitic violence in Boston. "My name is just as Irish as that of Judge Walsh and I have a notion that every fair-minded person of the *same strain* is burning with righteous indignation," Dineen warned. "That kind of a decision [the conviction of Hodas and Blaustein] does not help the cause of tolerance in Boston, nor is the cause of tolerance, of Americanism, of decency helped in any measure by the fact that a police sergeant on the Boston Police Department can beat up a prisoner, whether he be Jewish or Gentile, and get away with it."[119]

Addressing himself to the young people of Boston, Dineen reminded them that anti-Semitism "is the cornerstone of Fascism" that Hitler skillfully manipulated in his rise to power. Dineen concluded his impassioned broadcast by analyzing the ways in which anti-Semitism undermined fundamental American ideals and values.

> If you are a juvenile and if you've heard nasty things about the Jews from grownups, or from your teachers, tell your father about it, and ask him to do something about it. If he's not interested, write a letter to me about it and sign your name. Every time you listen to stories about Jews, and I mean unfavorable stories, critical stories, you're listening to Nazi propaganda, and, if you repeat those stories yourself, you're spreading Nazi propaganda, enemy propaganda....No matter what anybody tells you, there are Jewish boys, hundreds of thousands of them, fighting and dying in the U.S. Army, the Navy, the Marine Corps and the Air Force, so you can grow up in the kind of free world your fathers knew.[120]

Other voices in Irish Boston were raised in protest as well. Frances Sweeney, speaking for the Irish-American Defense Association and other liberal Irish Catholics, cited the lack of vision and absence of positive leadership in Irish Boston that helped to create an atmosphere conducive to hate and violence. "These attacks on Jewish children are the complete responsibility of Governor Saltonstall, Mayor Tobin, the church and clergy—all of whom have for three years buck-passed and ignored the tragedy," Sweeney argued. "These are not just assaults on Jewish children; they are a manifestation that the Christian Front still thrives and is encouraged in Boston. These attacks will lead to riots if their perpetrators are not arrested and jailed."[121]

Explicit manifestations of anti-Semitism dramatically decreased as a result of the public outcry and greater police vigilance. In a symbolic gesture of goodwill, Rabbi Herman H. Rubernovitz, president of the Boston Rabbinical Association, Rt. Rev. Monsignor Richard J. Haberlin, representing the Archdiocese of Boston, and Bishop G. Bromley Oxnam of the Methodist church denounced racism before twenty-five hundred people on the day following Thanksgiving.[122] The special investigation by the Massachusetts State Police into alleged police brutality in Boston found several members of the Boston Police Department guilty of assaults on Jews.[123] Governor Saltonstall fired Boston Police Commissioner Joseph T. Timilty.[124] Yet uneasy tensions characterized relations between Irish and Jews in Boston. The Boston correspondent of *Time* magazine perceptively saw the effects of ethnic conflict in the faces of the Irish and Jewish youth of Dorchester:

> There were still the Jews on Dorchester's Blue Hill Ave., living in inimical neighborhood to the Irish on Codman Sq. Jewish and Irish kids were still tense when they met. In a few years the city will be theirs, and it will be the same city of Irish and Jews and Yankees. But there was no one who really knew how to make them like to live together. The Governor seemed tired and drawn, the victorious Attorney General was still suspected of trying to "out Dewey Dewey," the ex-Police Commissioner was mending his fences for a comeback, and there was still the ugly tension in the fine faces of the kids of Dorchester.[125]

Like those strained expressions on the faces of the kids of Dorchester, bitterness lingered in Irish neighborhoods. Mayor Tobin criticized Frances Sweeney for "stirring up trouble."[126] Irish members of the Boston City Council remained as intransigent as the mayor over the existence of anti-Semitism in Boston. Once again the Boston Irish embraced a perspective in which defensiveness and rancor colored their perceptions of themselves, their place in Boston, and the role played by other ethnic groups.

BOSTON'S BITTER HERITAGE

In late December 1943, the two representatives of Boston's Jewish community in the city council, Councilors Charles I. Taylor and Isadore H. Muchnick, proposed the following resolution: "That the Boston City Council request the members of the Boston School Committee to register their approval to a plan already submitted to them for the purpose of arranging an educational program in the schools of Boston to eliminate racial discrimination."[127] Irish members of the city council dismissed the resolution. Councilor Michael L. Kinsella of South Boston illustrated this outlook: "Mr. Chairman, it seems to me that for some months past this question of discrimination has been a sore. It appears today that the question is brought out into public view more than ever before," Kinsella declared. "I am a member of a *minority race*, and if I don't know what discrimination is, at least my ancestors did, and I am not ready, as a member of the Boston City Council, to cast a vote that is predicated on the belief that discrimination does exist in Boston."[128]

The revelations of anti-Semitism in the 1940s and Irish-Jewish ethnic conflict in the public schools in the 1930s notwithstanding, Irish members of the city council refused to acknowledge the existence of discrimination in Boston. These representatives of Irish neighborhoods stridently refused to consider any positive program designed to lessen accumulating ethnic tensions in Boston's public schools. Like the stand taken by Mayor Tobin, the city council saw in the cry of discrimination an attempt to discredit the Boston Irish. Such a perspective was not new to Irish Boston. It reinforced the community's defensiveness and parochialism to be sure and illustrated the ghetto mentality that often characterized an Irish perspective during periods of tension. Hence the sons of Erin argued that the real victims of discrimination in Boston were not Jews, Blacks, or Italians, but the Irish! Councilor Mathew F. Hanley illustrated this outlook when he dismissed all the commotion about discrimination in Boston.

> Discrimination—that word has been used since the beginning of time, and it will be used until the consummation of time. There was no thought of or idea of anti-Semitism until that filthy mouth of the air-ways called this town or this city the city of bums. A reporter

from *P.M.* was the beginning, when he barged into a press confer-
ence of Governor Saltonstall, and was ejected, both verbally and
physically . . . . We are talking on something [discrimination] we are
amplifying something, that may grow like a prairie fire. The way to
put out a fire is to stop it at the beginning, and not allow it to envelop
a city, state or town. And, in conclusion, the City of Boston elected
twenty-two councilors to this Honorable Body, each and every one
of you educated to the philosophy of Americanism, but New York
City elected in the last election six of our Communists to the New
York City Council. And yet we are called the city of bums.[129]

Thus Councilors Michael L. Kinsella, Mathew F. Hanley, William
A. Carey, Thomas J. Hannon, Joseph M. Scannel, and Daniel F.
Sullivan argued that to acknowledge the existence of discrimination
in Boston was to condemn Irish Catholicism.[130] Discrimination
against Jews and Blacks was unthinkable in vew of the historic oppression of the Boston Irish. Charges of discrimination against Jews
in the face of their rapid upward socioeconomic mobility were simply absurd for these Irish representatives of South Boston and Dorchester. Turning to Councilors Taylor and Muchnick, Councilor
Kinsella replied:

I said in my remarks a few minutes ago that instead of being discriminated against, the path has been made easy for them [Jews] . . . .
And for the benefit of the other fourteen of fifteen members of this
Body, including the sponsor, let me say that a vote for this resolve or
order is a vote admitting the existence of a condition that, if you ask
me, has been very favorable to the class the gentleman represents
and I have the highest regard for them.[131]

The weight of the city's past socioeconomic frustrations and long-
standing resentments colored the outlook of Irish Boston during the
early years of the 1940s. When Councilors Taylor and Muchnick
once again introduced resolutions dealing with discrimination in
Boston in April 1944, the Irish members of the city council dismissed
such allegations as political rhetoric.[132] Once again these sons of
Erin stridently pointed to historic discrimination against the Irish as
evidence of the absence of discrimination against Jews and Blacks.[133]
Indeed, perceptions of social inferiority both real and imagined
characterized an Irish perspective during these years.

By mid-decade Irish and Jews were more estranged than ever before. The activities of Coughlinites, the Christian Front, and anti-
Semitic hoodlums helped to alienate Irish and Jews. But ethnic conflict in Boston was more complex than the overt actions of the com-
paratively small number of marginal individuals who engaged in
overt anti-Semitic terrorism. Less explicit manifestations of ethnic
conflict promoted an atmosphere conducive to misunderstanding,
bitterness, and distrust in many of Boston's Irish and Jewish neighborhoods. The force of the international system served as a catalyst
for the articulation of political, social, psychological, and cultural
grievances.

In a fundamental sense the outbursts of anti-Semitism in the 1940s
raised larger questions about the role of ethnicity in Boston. The
majority of Boston's Irish did not directly participate in overt acts
of anti-Semitism. The Christian Front drew its support from Irish
neighborhoods, to be sure, but these true believers were probably
marginal men and women looking for a cause—any cause—to vent
their frustrations and disappointments. However, there were inescapable Irish overtones to manifestations of anti-Semitism nonetheless. The seething sense of social inferiority expressed in the institutional structure of Irish Boston—political, religious, and socioeconomic—made it easy for the Boston Irish to dismiss the reality
of anti-Semitism just because Brahmins, liberals, and Jews opposed
it. Ethnic antagonisms in this setting conceivably expressed historic
group conflicts rather than systematic racial hatreds. In the absence
of a positive and constructive Irish world view, anti-Semitism grew
through neglect. Moreover, the heightening salience of the international system in the years immediately preceding American participation in World War II strained Irish-Jewish relations. Unquestionably, American involvement in World War II was a central
event in the outbreak of interethnic conflict in the Hub.

NOTES

1. "Annual Report of Hecht Neighborhood House, 1939-1940, June
12, 1940," Papers of Hecht Neighborhood House, American Jewish Historical Society, Waltham, Massachusetts.

2. Ibid.

3. Ibid.

4. *Jewish Advocate*, 3 May 1940.

5. Charles H. Trout, "Boston During the Great Depression 1928-1940" (Ph.D. diss., Columbia University, 1972), pp. 544-45.

6. Ibid., p. 544.

7. *Jewish Advocate*, 11 October 1940.

8. Ibid., 16 August 1940.

9. The Louis E. Kirstein Papers (Baker Library, Harvard University, Cambridge, Massachusetts), Case 5, reveal the intensive efforts that Boston's Jews launched on behalf of Jewish refugees in Europe.

10. *Jewish Advocate*, 22 March 1946; 27 September 1940; 18 July 1941; 12 September 1941.

11. "Annual Report, 1939-1940, June 12, 1940," Papers of Hecht Neighborhood House; *Jewish Advocate*, 13 September 1940; 20 September 1940; 6 December 1940.

12. *Jewish Advocate*, 23 August 1940.

13. Ibid.

14. Ibid., 2 August 1940.

15. Ibid., 19 January 1940; 1 March 1940; 15 March 1900; 30 August 1940; 7 June 1940; 26 June 1941; 10 October 1941; 31 October 1941; Boston, Mass., *Report of the Proceedings of the City Council of the City of Boston*, October 14, 1940, pp. 371-72; June 23, 1941, pp. 237-38; May 4, 1942, pp. 149-52 (hereafter cited as *City Council Proceedings*).

16. *Jewish Advocate*, 6 June 1941.

17. Ibid., 10 October 1941.

18. Ibid., 26 June 1941.

19. Louis E. Kirstein, Memorandum, Louis E. Kirstein Papers, Case 2.

20. *Jewish Advocate*, 21 March 1941.

21. Papers of Hecht Neighborhood House.

22. Boston, Mass., *Report of the Election Department of the City of Boston 1932-1944*; Trout, "Boston During the Great Depression," p. 605.

23. *Jewish Advocate*, 5 July 1940.

24. Ibid., 23 August 1940.

25. Ibid., 22 March 1940.

26. *City Council Proceedings*, December 20, 1943, pp. 395-403; April 3, 1944, pp. 170-78; see also Papers of Hecht Neighborhood House.

27. *Jewish Advocate*, 4 April 1941; 30 May 1941; 25 July 1941; *City Council Proceedings*, December 20, 1943, pp. 395-430; April 3, 1944, pp. 170-78.

28. *Jewish Advocate*, 12 December 1941.

29. Louis E. Kirstein, Memorandum, Louis E. Kirstein Papers, Case 5.

30. Trout, "Boston During the Great Depression," p. 548.

31. John P. Diggins, *Mussolini and Fascism, The View from America* (Princeton: Princeton University Press, 1972), p. 345.

32. Ibid., p. 345.

33. Ibid., p. 345.

34. *Gazzetta del Massachusetts*, 20 April 1940.

35. *Italian News*, 27 December 1940.

36. William F. Whyte, *Street Corner Society, The Social Structure of an Italian Slum* (Chicago: University of Chicago Press, 1943), p. 230.

37. *Italian News*, 5 July 1940.

38. Ibid., 25 April 1941; 2 May 1941; 9 May 1941.

39. Ibid., 9 May 1941.

40. Ibid., 15 August 1941.

41. Ibid., 11 July 1941.

42. *Gazzetta del Massachusetts*, 10 January 1942.

43. *Italian News*, 12 December 1941.

44. Diggins, *Mussolini and Fascism*, p. 351.

45. Ibid.

46. *New York Times*, 13 June 1940.

47. Ibid.

48. Ibid., 22 June 1940.

49. Ibid.

50. Ibid., 4 August 1941.

51. Ibid.

52. J. Joseph Huthmacher, *Massachusetts People and Politics 1919-1933* (Cambridge: Harvard University Press, 1959), p. 93.

53. *New York Times*, 4 May 1941.

54. Ibid., 15 August 1941, p. 3.

55. Ibid.

56. Congressman Joseph Martin Papers, "Neutrality, 1941," Box H-7, Stonehill College Archives, North Easton, Massachusetts. Unfortunately, the Congressman John W. McCormack Papers (Boston University, Boston, Massachusetts) do not deal in any detail with the views of constituents regarding international issues.

57. Congressman Joseph Martin Papers, "Neutrality, 1941."

58. Ibid.

59. Ibid.

60. *New York Times*, 7 December 1940.

61. Ibid., 8 December 1940.

62. Ibid.

63. Ibid. (emphasis added).

64. Congressman Joseph Martin Papers, "Neutrality, 1941."

65. *Boston Pilot*, 27 January 1940.

66. Ibid. (emphasis added).

67. Ibid., 3 February 1940.

68. Ibid., 12 July 1941.

69. Ibid., 15 March 1941.

70. *New York Times*, 4 March 1941, p. 9.

71. *Boston Pilot*, 18 January 1941.

72. Ibid., 20 September 1941.

73. Ibid.

74. Ibid., 13 December 1941.

75. Because anti-Semitism is no longer a respectable prejudice, the full extent of organized anti-Semitic activities is difficult to assess. During my research I encountered virtual silence concerning anti-Semitism among members of Boston's Irish and Jewish communities. Consequently, a number of extensive newspaper files housed at the Anti-Defamation League, New York, N.Y., serves as the primary documentary evidence. There was great reluctance on the part of Boston's major metropolitan dailies except the *Christian Science Monitor* even to print news stories about anti-Semitic activities. Unfortunately, the full story of anti-Semitism in Boston during the 1940s may never be revealed. The Boston Police Department contends that police blotters, arrest records, patterns of ethnic street violence, and so on that would presumably document anti-Semitic activities are "no longer available," personal letter, 22 July 1976, from Stephen P. Dunleavy, confidential secretary to the Police Commissioner, to author.

76. William V. Shannon, *The American Irish* (New York: Macmillan Co., 1963), p. 317.

77. Ibid.

78. Newspaper clipping, 12 June 1941, A.D.L. Files, Box 11, Anti-Defamation League of B'nai B'rith, New York, N.Y. (hereafter cited as A.D.L. Files).

79. Ibid.

80. Shannon, *The American Irish*, p. 317.

81. Ibid., p. 318; for analyses of the activities of the Christian Front see: Charles J. Tull, *Father Coughlin and the New Deal* (Syracuse, N.Y.: Syracuse University Press, 1965), pp. 189-91; Sheldon Marcus, *Father Coughlin, The Tumultous Life of the Priest of the Little Flower* (Boston: Little, Brown & Co., 1973), pp. 157-58; Ronald H. Bayor, *Neighbors in Conflict, The Irish, Germans, Jews, and Italians of New York City, 1929-1941* (Baltimore: John Hopkins University Press, 1978), pp. 98-99, 101-106.

82. *Boston Traveler*, 29 October 1940, A.D.L. Files, Box 11; Louis E.

Kirstein Papers, Case 5; Dr. Joshua Loth Leibman to O'Connell, 21 April 1943; William Henry O'Connell Papers, Archives of the Archdiocese of Boston, Brighton, Massachusetts.

83. *Boston Traveler*, 29 October 1940, A.D.L. Files, Box 11.

84. Newspaper Clippings, 3 June 1941, and 12 June 1941, A.D.L. Files, Box 11.

85. Ibid.

86. Ibid.

87. Lawrence J. McCaffrey, *The Irish Diaspora in America* (Bloomington: Indiana University Press, 1976), pp. 78-79.

88. *Boston Traveler*, 29 October 1940, A.D.L. Files, Box 11.

89. Ibid.

90. *P.M.*, 15 March 1942, A.D.L. Files, Box 6.

91. Newspaper Clipping, 15 March 1942, ibid.

92. Ibid.

93. Ibid.

94. Ibid.

95. *Boston Globe*, 16 March 1942, ibid.

96. Ibid.

97. Ibid.

98. Ibid.

99. Ibid.

100. Ibid.

101. Newspaper Clipping, undated, A.D.L. Files, Box 43.

102. *Boston Globe*, 17 October 1943, ibid.

103. *Christian Science Monitor*, 19 October 1943, A.D.L. Files, Box 13.

104. Ibid.

105. Newspaper Clipping, 19 October 1943, A.D.L. Files, Box 43.

106. Ibid.

107. *Christian Science.Monitor*, 20 October 1943, ibid.

108. Ibid.

109. Ibid. (emphasis added).

110. Ibid. (emphasis added).

111. *P.M.*, 21 October 1943, ibid.

112. Ibid. Members of the committee included: Judges Harold P. Williams and Abraham L. Pinanski of the Massachusetts Superior Court; Judge Jacob J. Kaplan, retired special justice in Roxbury District Court; Rev. Robert P. Barry; and Rabbi Joshua L. Liebman.

113. *P.M.*, 21 October 1943, A.D.L. Files, Box 43.

114. Ibid.

115. Ibid.

116. "A Catholic Views With Indignation Recent Events in the Hub," 27 November 1943, ibid.

117. Ibid.

118. "Jews Terrorized in Boston," 20 October 1943, ibid.

119. "A Catholic Views With Indignation Recent Events in the Hub," 27 November 1943, ibid. (emphasis added).

120. Ibid. (emphasis added).

121. Newspaper Clipping, "Jews Terrorized by Hoodlums in Boston," 22 October 1943, ibid.

122. *P.M.*, 29 November 1943, ibid. In the spring of 1943, Cardinal O'Connell called anti-Semites "Unchristian hoodlums" and described anti-Semitism as "spiritual hoodlumism." But O'Connell's pronouncements were often too little, too late. See, for example, the letter from Dr. Joshua Loth Leibman of Boston's Temple Israel to O'Connell, 21 April 1943; William Henry O'Connell Papers.

123. *New York Post*, 11 November 1943, A.D.L. Files, Box 43.

124. *New York Post*, 26 November 1943, ibid.

125. *P.M.*, "Letters From the Editor," 3 November 1943, ibid.

126. *P.M.*, 3 November 1943, ibid.

127. *City Council Proceedings*, December 20, 1943.

128. Ibid., p. 395 (emphasis added).

129. Ibid., p. 401.

130. Ibid., pp. 398-403.

131. Ibid., p. 398.

132. Ibid., April 3, 1944, pp. 170-78.

133. Ibid., pp. 170-78.

6

Conclusions:
Ethnicity and International
Politics in Boston

Ethnic conflict in Boston resulted from the concatenation of three sets of circumstances. The first was the socioeconomic upheavals of the depression, which produced disorientation and heightened insecurities in Irish, Italian, and Jewish neighborhoods. The second was the historical patterns of interethnic relations in Boston. These included the city's political system, socioeconomic institutions, and cultural cleavages that dated back to the Irish arrival in the 1840s. Irish-Yankee antagonisms throughout the nineteenth and early twentieth centuries introduced a rigidity and defensiveness into ethnic relations among Irish and Yankees and later immigrant groups. Although the Jews escaped the most negative effects of these cleavages, Irish, Italians, and Yankees were preoccupied by them. In this setting, conflict was institutionalized, resulting in strained interethnic relations. Although conflict among competing groups over scarce resources is natural, ethnicity in Boston too often began from a "we-they" perspective. This engendered conflict, reducing the likelihood of compromise or the abatement of hostility. The third factor was the impact of the international system of the 1930s and 1940s, which served as a catalyst for the articulation of ethnic grievances in a setting of already acute frustrations. Thus all three sets of factors were necessary for the realization of ethnic conflict between 1935 and 1944. These variables suggest the complexity of interethnic relations in Boston.

THE ITALIANS

Italian and Irish neighborhoods were among the hardest hit areas of the city during the years of the depression. Although Jews and Yankees were also affected negatively, it was the Italians and Irish who underwent intense economic suffering. Their disadvantaged position on the lowest rungs of Boston's socioeconomic ladder during times of prosperity resulted in massive unemployment, alienation, and frustration during the depression. Ethnic solidarities, consequently, increased.

Initially, ethnicity strengthened pride and self-respect. During a period of socioeconomic upheaval and insecurity, ethnic identities served as a constructive outlet for group fears and suspicions. But the historic salience of ethnicity in Boston, combined with rising tensions during the mid 1930s, accentuated differences among groups. The economic, social, and psychological strains of the depression produced an atmosphere contributing to further ethnic polarizations. As the depression deepened, Boston's Italians like the Irish retreated behind ghetto walls, "eyeing outsiders with suspicion."[1]

The salience of ethnic ties increased in the Italian neighborhoods of the West End, the North End, and East Boston. The very stability of Italian neighborhoods that had acted as a barrier to the outside world since 1900 further isolated the Italian community from intercourse with the rest of the city during the depression. Other forces promoted the assertion of Italian ethnicity as well. Irish discrimination in politics and the administration of the church, Brahmin-Yankee socioeconomic prejudice, and the omnipresence of an alien (Irish) municipal bureaucracy reinforced social distance between the North End and the city beyond. When the international system dramatically intruded into the West End, North End, and East Boston in 1935, ethnic conflict resulted.

The Italian war in Ethiopia served as a catalyst for the articulation of long-standing ethnic grievances. The intense demonstrations on behalf of Mussolini's victories in Ethiopia constituted a search for a meaningful Italian American ethnic identity. Xenophobia and nativism had taken their toll on Italian neighborhoods in Boston. The memory of Sacco and Vanzetti lingered among the twisted cobblestone streets and crowded neighborhoods of the

North End. To be of Italian ancestry in the 1930s, therefore, constituted a profound identity crisis. Political, socioeconomic, and cultural acceptance as full American citizens seemed an unreachable
goal. The vision of a resurgent Italy was of inestimable value in
heightening ethnic pride and self-esteem. Under the charismatic
leadership of Benito Mussolini, Italy at last was making its mark in
the world. Boston's Italians by virtue of their cultural, ancestral,
and familial ties to Italy shared in this new and exciting vision.
Throughout the 1930s and the first years of the 1940s, Italy's global
stance cast a pervasive shadow over Italian Boston.

The frenzied demonstrations supporting Italian victories in
Ethiopia, the generous financial support Mussolini received, and
the intensive lobbying efforts undertaken to halt revision of the
American neutrality acts illustrated the tremendous power that
Mussolini exerted over the minds and hearts of Boston's Italian
community. In providing the residents of the West End, North End,
and East Boston with pride and self-respect, Mussolini's Italy gained
their affection and enthusiasm. Through their support for Italy's
war aims, Italian Americans clashed with Boston's Blacks and Jews.
The racial epithets that Boston's Italian press hurled at Blacks and
Jews were a principal manifestation of the role of the international
system in provoking direct ethnic conflict in Boston. So, too, were
the spontaneous demonstrations denouncing Haile Selassie and his
Black troops. Indeed, Italian antipathies toward Blacks and to a
lesser extent Jews represented a sustained catharsis. Renewed ethnic
pride heightened dissatisfaction with life in Boston. In a fundamental sense, the emergence of Italian chauvinisms and profascist
activities were expressions of the cumulative effects of Italian prejudice in Boston. The Italo-Ethiopian War gave expression to the
isolation and bitterness that years of economic hardships brought
to a head. Support for Italy, therefore, temporarily filled a void
and soothed a chronic wound in the identities of Boston's Italian
American community.

Several factors mitigated the full fury of Italian-Black and
Italian-Jewish conflict, however. Boston's small Black community
of the South End was physically removed from the large Italian enclaves in the West End, East Boston, and the North End. The direct
and often vicious physical confrontations between Italians and

Blacks in Harlem did not occur in Boston.[2] Similarly, Boston's Italian and Jewish communities were also isolated from each other. Unlike Italian-Jewish conflict in New York City, Boston's Italians and Jews were not direct economic competitors.[3] Demographic factors and the absence of Italian-Jewish ecomonic competition lessened explicit instances of ethnic conflict in the Hub.

Thus the convergence of international and domestic systems explains the principal dynamics of ethnic conflict in Boston. The institutional completeness of Italian Boston—its high degree of spatial segregation, low rates of upward socioeconomic mobility, political isolation, and cultural alienation—influenced the way that Boston's Italian community reacted to the ongoing international system. The strength of ethnic ties with Italy and the absence of a satisfactory American identity during the depression set the stage; the direct impact of the international system defined the specific forms of ethnic conflict. If sustained manifestations of ethnic conflict were somewhat rare in Italian neighborhoods, bitterness nonetheless lingered in Boston. Irish frustrations and defensiveness amplified this uneasiness. Once again the convergence of domestic and international systems resulted in ethnic conflict.

THE IRISH

A seething sense of perceived social inferiority pervaded South Boston throughout the twentieth century. In many respects Boston sharply contrasted with other cities with large Irish populations. Unlike New York, Philadelphia, and Chicago, the Boston Irish never conquered the city. With time the Boston Irish built a formidable organization that challenged explicit Brahmin-Yankee hegemony in politics on a local level. However, the city's financial direction, corporate wealth, socioeconomic mobility, and cultural predominance remained firmly in Brahmin hands. In many ways Boston was as Brahmin in 1940 as it had been one hundred years earlier when the Irish first began to arrive in large numbers. Beacon Hill, the Back Bay, the Public Gardens, Henry Hobson Richardson's Trinity church, and, of course, Harvard University were tremendously evocative symbols to the Irish of South Boston, Roxbury, and Dorchester. Indeed the economic and social in-

stability of the depression only accentuated the force of these ubiquitous and foreboding symbols of Yankee success, power, and
prestige. The historic struggle between Irish and Brahmins condi-
tioned the Boston Irish to view "their" city and the world around
them from a ghettoized perspective. The influx of Jews and Italians
in the late nineteenth and twentieth centuries (and the attendant
ethnic rivalries that followed in jobs, housing, the church, politics,
and city government) heightened the Irish tendency to view the
world from the "we-they" perspective. This tendency only increased during the years of economic and social upheavals of the
1930s. The Boston Irish confronted the world of the mid 1930s with
less than perfect living conditions—high rates of joblessness, a
chronic inability to achieve upward socioeconomic mobility, and
deteriorating neighborhoods. In this dismal atmosphere past ethnic
animosities surfaced while new hostilities emerged. Like the Italians
of the North End and East Boston, the Boston Irish were preoccupied by international politics in direct and tangible ways.

The impact of international issues and events resulted in ethnic
conflict between the Boston Irish and Jews and the Irish and liberal
Brahmin-Yankees. Through their vehement anticommunism, isolationism, and Anglophobia, the Boston Irish vented long-standing
ethnic grievances. The victories of atheistic "communism" in Mexico
and Spain became something of a self-fulfilling prophecy in Irish
sections. It proved that anti-Catholic bigotry and hate were as rampant in the international system as they were in the United States.
Anglophobia indulged traditional Irish Catholic hatred of all things
British. Through isolationism, the Boston Irish demonstrated the
"Americanism" of their allegiance to the United States. In their
preoccupation with anticommunism, Anglophobia, and isolationism, the Boston Irish vented their dissatisfaction with American
life. The ghettoized world view of Irish Boston generated Irish-
Jewish and Irish-WASP conflict.

The most virulent manifestations of Irish hostility toward Jews
resulted in outbursts of anti-Semitism in the 1940s. Undoubtedly,
the Detroit radio priest Father Charles E. Coughlin promoted a
climate of hate and bitterness in a few Irish neighborhoods. In 1935
Coughlin tied his racist diatribes to the deteriorating international
system. By 1940 Coughlin's fascist-inspired organization the Chris-

tian Front had a following in South Boston, Roxbury, and Dorchester. The organized character of anti-Semitism between 1942 and 1944 suggested the participation of Coughlin's true believers. But the role of Coughlinite groups illustrated only one aspect of Irish ethnic conflict in Boston.

Without a doubt, the lack of constructive ethnic leadership in Boston's Irish community facilitated the outbursts of anti-Jewish and antiliberal hysteria in the 1940s. The church, socioeconomic elites, and the political establishment of Irish Boston embraced a strident and shrill defensiveness that the impact of the international system—particularly communist inroads in Mexico and Spain, the Spanish Civil War, and the end of American isolationism—brought to a frenzied pitch. Rather than promoting an outlook that emphasized the common humanity of all persecuted peoples, the leadership of Irish Boston felt compelled to assert a sort of collective whine—emphasizing over and over again the slights and insensitivities of liberal American Jews and WASPS towards the sufferings of Irish Catholics. Cardinal O'Connell, the editors of the *Boston Pilot*, David I. Walsh, James Michael Curley, and a host of lesser lights hammered home the same theme. These leaders often expressed their own ethnic insecurities while pandering to the fears of their followers. In each case from red-baiting to Jew-baiting, Irish Catholic rancor expressed the ghettoization of the Boston Irish. This minority consciousness was a positive barrier to the maturation of a more constructive Irish ethnic identity throughout the 1930s and 1940s.

Socioeconomic frustrations also animated Irish animosities in Boston. The Irish of South Boston, Roxbury, and Dorchester sullenly perceived the upward socioeconomic mobility of the Hub's Jewish community. The relocation of Boston's Jewish community during the first years of the 1930s in Roxbury, Dorchester, and Mattapan displaced Irish residents exacerbating tensions. Unlike the lack of contact between Italians and Blacks and Italians and Jews, Boston's Irish daily collided with the city's growing lower-middle-class Jewish neighborhoods.

In this complex setting, ethnic rivalries and competition helped to promote a climate in which ethnic conflict would flourish. The majority of the Boston Irish were not anti-Semitic. Clearly they overwhelmingly chose F.D.R. rather than Father Coughlin in 1936. The 72 percent of the vote that Roosevelt received in South Boston in 1944 was still a landslide despite the almost 20 percent defection since 1932. But the long-established patterns of ethnic conflict in the nineteenth and twentieth centuries (Irish vs. Brahmin-Yankee and Irish vs. Italians and Jews) predisposed the Boston Irish to be against something just because Brahmins, liberals, and Jews were for it.[4] In other words, the Boston Irish were reacting to what they perceived as a position of social inferiority.[5] Historic group fears, socioeconomic frustrations, and cultural alienation, exacerbated by the direct impact of a chaotic international system, produced Irish-Jewish and Irish-WASP ethnic conflict in Boston. Thus isolation-ism, anticommunism, and Anglophobia tended to heighten already existing ethnic tensions by legitimizing more subtle anti-Jewish and anti-WASP stereotypes within the larger Irish community. The tragedy of Irish Boston during the 1930s and 1940s, therefore, was not in the increasing salience of ethnicity, but the profoundly negative manifestations that it assumed.

THE JEWS

A deteriorating international system provided Boston's Jews with demonstrable proof of the necessity of ethnic pluralism in the 1930s and 1940s. Indeed, the specter of worldwide anti-Semitism, Nazism, and fascism heightened Jewish ethnic identities in Boston. Consequently, Boston's Jewish community mobilized to oppose all forms of anti-Semitism in the Hub. In addition, Boston Jewry vig-orously supported Zionism as the only permanent solution to the problem of European anti-Semitism. In their opposition to anti-Semitism and fascism in the United States or Europe, Boston's Jews illustrated the strength of ethnic attachments. Moreover, the in-creasing support accorded the Zionist cause in Boston between 1935 and 1944 documented the tangible impact of the international system on Jewish ethnicity in Boston. Accelerating patterns of eth-nic conflict placed great strain on an evolving Jewish identity, how-ever. Ultimately these tensions were resolved in the strengthening of a Jewish commitment to political liberalism in Boston.

The international system had a significant impact on the development of Boston's Jewish community. The course of European anti-Semitism convinced Boston's Jews that the only defense against totalitarianism in the United States was an active and informed electorate committed to democratic principles. The *Jewish Advocate*, Hecht House, the Associated Jewish Philanthropies, and communal leaders Louis Kirstein, David Niles, Ben Selekman, and Rabbi Harry Levi repeatedly reaffirmed the necessity of a Jewish commitment to American liberalism. The lessons of Nazi Germany were clear. Any manifestations of religious and racial intolerence threatened the very foundations of a democratic state. A Jewish commitment to political liberalism steadily increased throughout the 1930s and 1940s. By 1944 Boston's Jews were the most articulate and steadfast supporters of the New Deal in Boston. Unquestionably, Roosevelt's policies particularly in foreign policy resulted in massive Jewish support.

It was the specter of victorious fascism throughout the world that did the most to heighten Jewish ethnicity in Boston. Irish support for isolationism, anticommunism, and Anglophobia particularly in the 1940s reemphasized the differences between Irish and Jews. Boston's Jews saw in the outbursts of anti-Semitism in Irish neighborhoods tangible evidence of the interplay between the international system and life in Boston. The intensity of Jewish opposition to manifestations of Irish anti-Semitism occasionally threatened a Jewish commitment to liberal ideals although several factors mitigated explicit Jewish antipathies to the Irish.

The institutional structure of Jewish Boston limited the intensity of Jewish hostilities. The *Jewish Advocate*, Hecht House, and the Associated Jewish Philanthropies refused to lash out at Irish or Italian insensitivities in a destructive way. These institutions refused to exploit the fears and prejudices of Boston's Jewish community. This orientation stood in contrast to the defensiveness, isolation, and alienation that the leadership of Boston's Irish and Italian communities regularly exploited. The self-conscious attempt to embrace political liberalism gave expression to a constructive Jewish identity. This orientation illustrated a kind of secular messianism that found expression in a Jewish commitment to liberal political and social ideals in Boston—civil rights, the welfare state, philanthropic endeavors. Thus Jewish liberalism further heightened cultural differences among Boston's other ethnic groups. In their cognizance of the international and domestic manifestations of anti-Semitism and fascism, Boston's Jewish community sought a re-affirmation of the integrity of the ethnic group and its compatibility with American values and ideals. Thus the self-conscious pursuit of democratic values represented political, socioeconomic, and cul-tural transitions that were taking hold of the Jewish community. Rather than retreating behind ghetto walls, Boston's Jews tried to deal constructively with tensions between political ideals and do-mestic and international realities.

ETHNICITY AND INTERNATIONAL POLITICS

Four issues need to be raised concerning the conceptual thrust of this study. First, the relationships between social class and ethnicity need to be clarified. For Boston's Irish and Italians, social class in-cluded more than just economic attributes such as income or occu-pation. Throughout nineteenth- and twentieth-century Boston, social class had been colored by ethnicity. This may have strength-ened the salience of ethnicity in Boston as opposed to other cities like Denver or San Francisco. Undoubtedly, Boston's Irish and Italians during the 1930s were reacting to what they perceived as a position of social inferiority. Although their chronically depressed socioeconomic status contributed to this outlook, ethnic an-tagonisms were also significant. This condition is best illustrated in the " 'damned Harvard bastards!' mentality (an alleged remark of a Boston monsignor to another when John Kennedy rode by him in a St. Patrick's day parade)."[6] In such an environment, it was easy to be against something just because the other guy was for it.[7]

Second, the precise manifestations of ethnic conflict in Boston were not static variables. Specific spatial temporal conditions de-fined the relations between Irish, Italians, and Jews and these were subject to change. Thus it would be interesting to speculate what would have happened in Boston had the economic hardships of the depression or the foreign problems of the 1930s been missing. Per-haps the reason the conflict has abated since the 1940s is that these factors were no longer present.

Third, this study underscores the transnational nature of ethnic conflict in Boston between 1935 and 1944. Three aspects of transnational interactions need to be emphasized. The first was the transfer of information, beliefs, and ideas from the international system to Boston's ethnic enclaves. Second, Boston's Irish, Italians, and Jews transformed international events into concrete issues and problems. Hence the transfer of information, ideas, and beliefs achieved tangible expression in ethnic conflict in Boston. Third, the preoccupation of Boston's ethnic groups with international issues and events in turn resulted in direct and indirect inputs into the international system frequently through foreign policy processes.

Thus Boston's Irish, Italians, and Jews interacted with the international system for almost a decade precisely because these ethnic groups perceived that the international system was affecting vital interests. Boston's Jewish community, for example, contributed large amounts of money that helped to support the work of world Zionism, aided Jewish refugees, and provided food and medical assistance for European Jews. In each instance, Jewish ethnicity in Boston served as a direct input into the international system. Further examples of the interactions between the international system and Boston's ethnic groups were evident in Boston's Italian and Irish communities as well. Italian Americans vigorously attempted to thwart revision of the American neutrality laws when it appeared likely that such revisions would interfere with the Italian war effort in Ethiopia. These sustained attempts to influence American foreign policy obviously transcended the geographical confines of Boston. Similarly, Irish preoccupation with anticommunism, isolationism, and Anglophobia had important foreign policy implications. On occasion, it appeared likely that these Irish outlooks would threaten the realization of several foreign policy goals: rapprochement with the Soviet Union, aid to Great Britain, and military assistance to the Allies. Franklin D. Roosevelt and other members of the New Deal looked upon Senator David I. Walsh and William Cardinal O'Connell as powerful obstructionists.[8] Indeed, Senator Walsh's commanding position in the United States Senate guaranteed the Boston Irish some leverage on American foreign relations. All of these examples of the interactions flowing between the ongoing international system and Boston's ethnic enclaves emphasized the transnational dimensions of ethnicity in Boston.

A final issue remains unresolved in this study: how representative was ethnic conflict in Boston during the 1930s and 1940s for other cities throughout the United States? The data seem to indicate that the tendency to generalize from the case of Boston must be tempered. While a recent study of ethnic conflict in New York— Ronald Bayor's *Neighborhoods in Conflict*—supports a number of findings of this study, Boston had some unique features. The first was the pervasive influence of America's only urban aristocrats— the Brahmins. Indeed, the dominance of Unitarianism among the Brahmins frequently made them appear anti-Christian to many Irish and Italian Catholics. These cleavages spilled over into almost every significant area of life in Boston on both personal and institutional levels. The second was the dominance of the Catholic church in local politics. This was avoided in New York by the large Jewish population, in Pittsburgh by the large German Lutheran population, and in many other American cities by the huge Black in-migrations among the immigrant populations. Third, the dramatic differences in socioeconomic mobility for Irish and Italian Catholics in Boston and Irish and Italian Catholics nationally during the same period suggest that Boston was indeed different from many other American cities. Although the nature of ethnicity in Boston may well have differed from other American cities, this recognition does not necessarily lead one to assume that world politics during the 1930s and 1940s was any less important for San Francisco's Jews or Chicago's Irish. Indeed, this study argues that ethnicity and world politics are more interdependent than many scholars have heretofore suggested. This is a researchable question that may reveal more information concerning the transnational dynamics of ethnicity and the ethnic dimensions of world politics.

EPILOGUE: STIRRINGS OF CHANGE

The years between 1935 and 1944 represented a period of intense strain from both international and domestic perspectives. The social and economic upheavals of the depression years converged with the insecurity and uncertainty of a chaotic international system. The interaction between domestic and international conditions resulted in ethnic conflict making Boston a symbol of international conflict. The salience of ethnicity increased for each ethnic group during these difficult years. In a sense, the patterns of ethnic conflict in Boston—Irish, Italian, and Jewish—constituted a search for self-identity in collective and personal ways. This study explored the different manifestations of ethnicity and ethnic conflict that resulted during those years.

The quest for a meaningful ethnic self-identity did not stop with the conclusion of World War II. The specific conditions that resulted in ethnic conflict in the 1930s and 1940s disappeared in the post-World War II era, however. The winds of change were blowing even in the parochial environs of Irish Boston. The war experience broadened the visions and expectations of tens of thousands of Boston Irishmen. In many respects an era had ended. James Michael Curley's turbulent fifty years in Boston's politics were coming to a close. David I. Walsh's retirement from politics was at hand. William Cardinal O'Connell died in 1944. Amid the changing of the guard, newer voices and perspectives were asserted.

The Boston Irish responded to many of these voices. Archbishop Richard J. Cushing pioneered the ecumenism so badly needed in Boston. The bridges he built between Irish and Jews and Irish and Brahmin-Yankees eventually helped to heal some of the old wounds. In politics new voices also called for change. In his first electoral contest, John F. Kennedy challenged the Boston Irish in the 11th Congressional District to embrace new visions. Kennedy appealed to a national identity rather than a local one. His explicit appeal to World War II veterans during that campaign illustrated the changing forces within Boston's Irish community. He celebrated not the parochialisms of the past but the promise of the future—a future in which Irish ethnic identities would not only embrace parochial allegiances but national visions. Accelerating patterns of upward socioeconomic mobility, middle-class status, and higher levels of educational achievements helped to transform Irish Boston in the postwar period. The 1930s and 1940s, therefore, stand as a watershed in the history of Boston, symbolizing the end of one era, signifying the beginning of another. Ethnic conflicts would reoccur but never as intensely or as fanatically. The insularity of Italian and Irish neighborhoods lessened. By 1948 many of Boston's ethnic enclaves were "losing both their political clout and ethnic distinctiveness."[9] Boston's Jews entirely abandoned the city while thousands of Irish and Italians moved to the suburbs. The quest for ethnic self-identity continued, of course, particularly in periods of social and economic unrest. Despite the crucial problems that the city faced in the postwar period, it would not experience again the years of turbulence and turmoil in which Boston became a symbol of international conflict.

NOTES

1. Charles H. Trout, "Boston During the Great Depression 1928-1940" (Ph.D. diss., Columbia University, 1972), p. 45.

2. John P. Diggins, *Mussolini and Fascism, The View from America* (Princeton: Princeton University Press, 1972), p. 537.

3. Ronald H. Bayor, "Italians, Jews and Ethnic Conflict," *International Migration Review* 6 (Winter 1972): 388.

4. Andrew M. Greeley, January 21, 1977, personal letter.

5. Ibid., February 7, 1977.

6. Ibid., January 26, 1977.

7. Ibid.

8. Trout, "Boston During the Great Depression," p. 532.

9. Thomas H. O'Connor, *Bibles, Brahmins, and Bosses, A Short History of Boston* (Boston: Trustees of the Boston Public Library of the City of Boston, 1976), p. 126.

Selected Bibliography

A NOTE ON THE SOURCES

This study benefits from various important sources of data. The analysis of Boston's Irish and Jewish communities draws heavily on several manuscript collections. The Archives of the Archdiocese of Boston offers key insights into perhaps the most significant institution of Boston's Irish community—the Catholic church and its influential leader William Cardinal O'Connell. O'Connell aimed at erecting a stable bureaucratic organization that would touch the lives of hundreds of thousands of Catholics. The William Henry O'Connell Papers (Archives of the Archdiocese of Boston, Brighton, Massachusetts) are a rich depository of data. The Massachusetts State Archives at the Massachusetts State Library houses manuscript collections dealing with Boston politics, particularly Irish anticommunism. The Congressman Joseph Martin Papers (Stonehill College Archives, North Easton, Massachusetts) offer data on Irish isolationism throughout the period.

Several manuscript collections helped me in my search for data on Boston's Jewish community. The Papers of Hecht Neighborhood House (American Jewish Historical Society, Waltham, Massachusetts) constitute a record of how one of Boston's principal Jewish organizations responded to the domestic and international events of the 1930s and 1940s. The Louis E. Kirstein Papers (Baker Library, Harvard University, Cambridge, Massachusetts) document the involvement of Boston's Jewish leadership in liberal politics, opposition to anti-Semitism, and support for philanthropic endeavors. Several newspaper files at the Anti-Defamation League of B'nai B'rith (New York, N.Y.) were invaluable sources of data on anti-Semitism in Boston. Unfortunately, I could locate no archival collections dealing with Boston's Italian community.

Boston's ethnic press was another crucial source of data in the life of Irish, Italian, and Jewish neighborhoods. These newspapers not only attempted to influence the formation of public opinion but provided a continuing commentary on how the city's Irish, Italians, and Jews responded to the domestic and foreign problems of the 1930s and 1940s. The analysis of newspapers cannot take the place of sophisticated attitudinal surveys of public opinion, but they nonetheless provide insight into the dynamics of ethnicity in Boston. Five newspapers constituted the most important sources of data: the *Boston Pilot*, the *Gazzetta del Massachusetts*, the *Guardian*, the *Italian News*, and the *Jewish Advocate*. Several other newspapers were consulted as well: the *Boston Globe*, the *Boston Traveler*, the *Christian Science Monitor*, and the *New York Times*. The New York daily *P.M.* frequently reported on anti-Semitism in Boston during the 1940s. The weekly editions of *Social Justice* document Father Coughlin's increasingly confused thought on domestic and international politics until it was ordered closed by the U.S. Justice Department in 1942 for its seditious activities. Although the pages of *Social Justice* reveal the full fury of Coughlin's invective, it is difficult to measure the extent of Coughlin's support in Boston and other cities throughout the United States.

Government documents, including Boston city and Massachusetts state documents and U.S. government documents, are a rich depository of data, particularly the *Report of the Election Department of the City of Boston, 1928-44; Report of the Proceedings of the City Council of the City of Boston, 1935-44; Report of the Proceedings of the School Committee of the City of Boston, 1935-44; and the Journal of the Massachusetts House, 1935-44*. In addition *The Census of Massachusetts, 1875-1895: Population and Social Statistics* and the successive volumes of the *Census of the United States* provide data on Boston's socioeconomic development.

There are a number of important unpublished studies dealing with ethnicity. Charles H. Trout, "Boston During the Great Depression 1928-1940" (Ph.D. diss., Columbia University, 1972), is an outstanding study of the impact of the depression on Boston's political, economic, social, and cultural institutions. Trout's study is elegantly written and meticulously researched. Rosalind Brill, "The Rise of Urban Liberalism: Boston City Politics, 1926-1933" (Senior honors thesis, Brandeis University, 1967), is a useful study. Gustave Serino, "Italians in the Political Life of Boston" (Ph.D diss., Harvard University, 1950), offers many insights into Italian alienation in Boston politics. William J. Grattan, "David I. Walsh and His Associates: A Study in Political Theory" (Ph.D. diss., Harvard University, 1958), and Thomas R. Mason, "Reform Politics in Boston: A Study of Ideology and Social Change in Municipal Government" (Ph.D. diss., Harvard University, 1963), are useful studies of Boston in the early years of the twentieth century.

There are many excellent historical studies of ethnicity in Boston. Oscar Handlin, *Boston's Immigrants, A Study in Acculturation*, rev. and enl. ed. (New York: Atheneum, 1970), is the classic account of Irish-Yankee relations in the nineteenth century. Handlin was one of the first historians to challenge the assimilationist biases of American social science. Thomas N. Brown, *Irish American Nationalism 1870-1890* (Philadelphia: J.B. Lippincott Co., 1966), is an excellent account of the transnational pull of ethnic identity during the last years of the nineteenth century. Brown's analysis of Irish ethnicity in Boston is insightful. Donna Merwick, *Boston Priests, 1848-1910, A Study in Social and Intellectual Change* (Cambridge: Harvard University Press, 1973), documents the increasing ethnic assertiveness of the Boston Irish by the turn of the twentieth century. Barbara M. Solomon presents an excellent study of immigrant restriction in the United States in *Ancestors and Immigrants, A Changing New England Tradition* (Cambridge: Harvard University Press, 1956), Solomon documents the complexity of interethnic relations in Boston amid the retrenchment of the Brahmins in the face of Irish politics and Italian and Jewish slums. Sam Bass Warner, Jr., *Streetcar Suburbs, The Process of Growth in Boston 1870-1900* (Cambridge: Harvard University Press and M.I.T. Press, 1962), reveals the fragmentation of Boston under the cumulative impact of technology.

There are some useful studies of ethnic politics in the twentieth century. J. Joseph Huthmacher, *Massachusetts People and Politics 1919-1933* (Cambridge: Harvard University Press, 1959), and Richard M. Abrams, *Conservatism in a Progressive Era, Massachusetts Politics 1920-1921* (Cambridge: Harvard University Press, 1964), document the increasing polarization between Irish and Yankees and the Irish and the newcomers—Italians and Jews. Lawrence Fuchs, *Political Behavior of American Jews* (Glencoe, Ill.: The Free Press, 1956), offers an insightful portrait of the uneasy relations between Irish and Jews in Boston politics. Samuel Lubell, *The Future of American Politics*, 3d ed. (New York: Harper & Row, 1963), supports Fuchs's contention of Irish-Jewish conflict. Three studies provide important overviews of the ethnic cleavages characteristic of Boston politics: Murray B. Levin, *The Alienated Voter, Politics in Boston* (New York: Holt, Rinehart & Winston, 1960); Alan Lupo, *Liberty's Chosen Home, The*

Politics of Violence in Boston (Boston: Little, Brown & Co., 1977); and Thomas H. O'Connor, *Bibles, Brahmins and Bosses, A Short History of Boston* (Boston: Trustees of the Boston Public Library of the City of Boston, 1976).

Sociological studies of ethnicity enrich the historical and political literature dealing with Boston. Robert A. Woods's pioneering studies of ethnicity in Boston during the late nineteenth and early twentieth centuries raised fundamental questions about immigrant adjustments to American life that have continued to preoccupy American sociologists throughout the twentieth century. In particular, *The City Wilderness* (Boston: Houghton, Mifflin & Co., 1898), and *Americans in Process, A Settlement Study* (Boston: Houghton, Mifflin & Co., 1902), are revealing accounts of the strains that waves of Italian and Jewish immigrants imposed on Boston. *The Zone of Emergence* (Cambridge: M.I.T. Press, 1962), a collaborative effort by Robert A. Woods and Albert J. Kennedy, is a striking account of working-class Irish neighborhoods in the first two decades of the twentieth century.

More contemporary sociological studies have continued to be preoccupied by questions of class and ethnicity. In this respect, *The Urban Villagers, Group and Class in the Life of Italian Americans* (New York: The Free Press, 1962), by Herbert Gans, provides several useful insights into the persistence of Italian identity in Boston despite his depreciation of the importance of ethnicity in favor of a class analysis. William F. Whyte, *Street Corner Society, The Social Structure of an Italian Slum* (Chicago: Chicago University Press, 1943), is a classic account of Italian ethnicity in Boston's North and West Ends in the 1940s. Whyte's participant-observer approach has been used well in Gerald D. Suttles, *The Social Order of the Slum, Ethnicity and Territory in the Inner City* (Chicago: University of Chicago Press, 1970). Suttles documents the crucial role that ethnic identity and territory play in a deteriorating inner-city neighborhood. His portrait of a small Italian neighborhood in transition is excellent.

For more generalized studies of ethnicity, Robert E. Park, *Race and Culture* (New York: The Free Press, 1945), and Louis Wirth, *The Ghetto* (Chicago: University of Chicago Press, 1928), are useful places to begin, despite their explicit assimilationist biases. The second edition of *Beyond the Melting Pot* (Cambridge: The M.I.T. Press, 1970), by Nathan Glazer and Daniel P. Moynihan, provides an interesting counterpoint to the omnipresent assimilationist biases of American sociology until the late 1960s. William M. Newman, *American Pluralism, A Study of Minority Groups and Social Theory* (New York: Harper & Row, 1973), is a fine critique of the literature up to 1973. The work of Andrew M. Greeley, especially *That*

Most Distressful Nation, The Taming of the American Irish (Chicago: Quadrangle Books, 1972); *Ethnicity in the United States: A Preliminary Reconnaissance* (New York: John Wiley & Sons, 1974); and *The American Catholic, A Social Portrait* (New York: Basic Books, 1977), provides the first systematic survey research data of non-Black and non-Hispanic ethnic groups in the United States. Greeley's analysis advances the study of the persistence of ethnicity in America.

The analysis of the global dimensions of ethnicity has steadily expanded in recent years. Students of ethnicity have tended to opt for less comprehensive conceptual statements than either R. A. Schermerhorn, *Comparative Ethnic Relations, A Framework for Theory and Research* (New York: Random House, 1970), or Tamotsu Shibutani and Kian Kawn, *Ethnic Stratification, A Comparative Approach* (New York: Macmillan Co., 1965). The work of Clifford Geertz in *The Interpretation of Cultures* (New York: Basic Books, 1972), and Harold Isaacs in *Idols of the Tribe, Group Identity and Political Change* (New York: Harper & Row, 1975), illustrate the significance of deeply felt ties in a variety of multiethnic societies throughout the world. Walker Connor's work especially "Nation-Building or Nation-Destroying," *World Politics* 24 (April 1972), and "The Politics of Ethnonationalism," *Journal of International Affairs* 27 (1973), helped to emphasize the critical role played by ethnicity in world politics, particularly in developing countries, despite the predominant assimilationist biases of the literature. *Internal Colonialism, The Celtic Fringe and British National Development, 1536-1966* (Los Angeles: University of California Press, 1975), by Michael Hechter, suggests the transnational dynamics of ethnicity through the elaboration of the concept of the international cultural division of labor. Ultimately, Hechter's analysis can be applied to global political and economic systems.

Several collections of essays have attempted to detail the international dimensions of ethnicity: Wendell Bell and Walter E. Freeman, eds., *Ethnicity and Nation-Building* (Beverly Hills: Sage Publications, 1974); Judy S. Bertelsen, ed., *Nonstate Nations in International Politics* (New York: Praeger, 1977); Leo A. Despres, ed., *Ethnicity and Resource Competition in Plural Societies* (The Hague: Mouton Publishers, 1975); Abdul A. Said and Luis R. Simmons, eds., *Ethnicity in an International Context* (New Brunswick, N.J.: Transaction Books, 1976); and Astri Suhrke and Lela Noble, eds., *Ethnic Conflict in International Relations* (New York: Praeger, 1978). For a penetrating and suggestive analysis of the interplay between ethnic groups and multinational corporations, see Cynthia H. Enloe, "Multinational Corporations in the Making and Unmaking of Ethnic Groups," in *Ethnonationalism, Multinational Corporations and the*

Modern State, ed. Ronald Grant and S. Wellhofer (Denver: University of Denver Monograph Series on World Affairs, 1979).

The concept of transnationalism has undergone considerable refinement in recent years. For a representative sample of the literature, see Karl Kaiser, "Transnational Politics: Toward a Theory of Multinational Politics," *International Organization* 25 (Autumn 1971); Robert O. Keohane and Joseph S. Nye, Jr., eds., *Transnational Relations and World Politics* (Cambridge: Harvard University Press, 1971); Samuel P. Huntington, "Transnational Organizations in World Politics," *World Politics* 25 (April 1973); and Robert O. Keohane and Joseph S. Nye, Jr., *Power and Interdependence* (Boston: Little, Brown & Co., 1976).

MANUSCRIPT COLLECTIONS

Boston, Mass. Boston University. Congressman John W. McCormack Papers.

Boston, Mass. Manuscripts Collection. Boston Public Library.

Boston, Mass. Massachusetts State Library. Massachusetts State Archives.

Brighton, Mass. Archives of the Archdiocese of Boston. William Henry O'Connell Papers.

Cambridge, Mass. Baker Library. Harvard University. Louis E. Kirstein Papers.

Cambridge, Mass. Harvard University Archives.

Newton, Mass. Boston College Archives.

New York, N.Y. American Irish Historical Society.

New York, N.Y. Anti-Defamation League of B'nai B'rith. Anti-Semitism in Boston.

New York, N.Y. New York Public Library. McKim-Maloney Papers.

North Easton, Mass. Stonehill College Archives. Congressman Joseph Martin Papers.

Waltham, Mass. American Jewish Historical Society. Papers of Hecht Neighborhood House.

Worcester, Mass. Holy Cross College. Senator David I. Walsh Papers.

NEWSPAPERS

Boston College Heights, 17 September 1935-1 January 1942.

Boston Pilot, 1 January 1935-1 January 1944.

Gazzetta del Massachusetts, 1 January 1935-1 January 1944.

Guardian, 1 January 1939-1 January 1944.
Italian News, 1 January 1939-1 January 1944.
Jewish Advocate, 1 January 1935-1 January 1944.
La Notizia, 1 January 1939-1 January 1940.
Newspaper Files: Anti-Defamation League of B'nai B'rith. Anti-Semitism
        in Boston. 1 January 1940-1 January 1948.
New York Times, 1 January 1940-1 January 1945.
Social Justice, 23 March 1936-15 April 1942.

GOVERNMENT DOCUMENTS

Boston City Documents. *Report of the Election Department of the City of
        Boston, 1928-44.*
Boston, Mass. *Report of the Proceedings of the City Council of the City of
        Boston, 1935-44.*
Boston, Mass. *Report of the Proceedings of the School Committee of the
        City of Boston, 1935-44.*
Commonwealth of Massachusetts. *Journal of the Massachusetts House,*
        1935-43.
Massachusetts Department of Commerce. *The Census of Massachusetts,
        1875: Population and Social Statistics,* vol. 1.
Massachusetts Department of Commerce. *The Census of Massachusetts,
        1895: Population and Social Statistics,* vol. 1.
U.S. Department of Commerce. Bureau of the Census. *Thirteenth Census
        of the United States, 1910: Population,* vol. 2.
U.S. Department of Commerce. Bureau of the Census. *Fourteenth Census
        of the United States, 1920: Population,* vol. 2.
U.S. Department of Commerce. Bureau of the Census, *Fifteenth Census of
        the United States, 1930: Population,* vol. 2.
U.S. Department of Commerce. Bureau of the Census. *Sixteenth Census of
        the United States, 1940: Population,* vol. 2

UNPUBLISHED STUDIES

Brill, Rosalind. "The Rise of Urban Liberalism: Boston City Politics, 1926-
        1933." Senior honors thesis, Brandeis University, 1967.
Grattan, William J. "David I. Walsh and His Associates: A Study in
        Political Theory." Ph.D. dissertation, Harvard University, 1958.
Mason, Thomas R. "Reform Politics in Boston: A Study of Ideology and
        Social Change in Municipal Government." Ph.D. dissertation,
        Harvard University, 1963.

Serino, Gustave. "Italians in the Political Life of Boston." Ph.D. dissertation,
    Harvard University, 1950.
Trout, Charles H. "Boston During the Great Depression 1928-1940." Ph.D.
    dissertation, Columbia University, 1972.

BOOKS

Abrams, Richard M. *Conservatism in a Progressive Era, Massachusetts
    Politics 1900-1921*. Cambridge: Harvard University Press, 1964.
Adler, Selig. *The Isolationist Impulse, Its Twentieth-Century Reaction*.
    London: Abelard-Schuman, 1957.
Almond, Gabriel A., and Verba, Sidney. *The Civic Culture, Political
    Attitudes and Democracy in Five Nations*. Boston: Little, Brown
    & Co., 1965.
Aron, Raymond. *Peace and War, A Theory of International Relations*.
    Translated by Richard Howard and Annette Baker Fox. Garden
    City, N.Y.: Doubleday, 1966.
Banfield, Edward C. *The Moral Basis of a Backward Society*. New York:
    The Free Press, 1958.
Banfield, Edward C., and Wilson, James Q. *City Politics*. Cambridge:
    Harvard University Press and M.I.T. Press, 1963.
Bayor, Ronald H. *Neighbors in Conflict, The Irish, Germans, Jews, and
    Italians of New York City, 1929-1941*. Baltimore: Johns Hopkins
    University Press, 1978.
Bell, J. Bowyer. *Besieged, Seven Cities Under Siege*. New York: Chilton
    Books, 1966.
Bell, Wendell, and Freeman, Walter E., eds. *Ethnicity and Nation-Building*.
    Beverly Hills: Sage Publications, 1974.
Bertelsen, Judy S., ed. *Nonstate Nations in International Politics*. New
    York: Praeger, 1977.
Blalock, Herbert. *Toward a Theory of Minority Group Relations*. New
    York: Capricorn Books, 1967.
Blodgett, Geoffrey. *The Gentle Reformers: Massachusetts Democrats in
    the Cleveland Era*. Cambridge: Harvard University Press, 1966.
Brown, Thomas N. *Irish American Nationalism 1870-1890*. Philadelphia:
    J.B. Lippincott Co., 1966.
Bryce, James. *The American Commonwealth*. 2 vols. New York: The
    Commonwealth Publishing Co., 1908.
Coughlin, Rev. Charles E. *Eight Lectures on Labor, Capital and Justice*.
    Royal Oak, Mich.: Radio League of the Little Flower, 1934.
_____. *Series of Lectures on Social Justice March 1935*. Royal Oak, Mich.:

The Radio League of the Little Flower, 1935.

_____. *16 Radio Lectures, 1938 Series.* Detroit: Condon Printing Co., 1938.

_____. *Why Leave Our Own? 13 Addresses on Christianity and Americanism January 8-April 2, 1939.* Detroit: The Inland Press, 1939.

Curley, James Michael. *I'd Do It Again.* Englewood Cliffs, N.J.: Prentice-Hall, 1957.

Despres, Leo A., ed. *Ethnicity and Resource Competition in Plural Societies.* The Hague: Mouton Publishers, 1975.

Devine, Robert A. *The Illusion of Neutrality, Franklin D. Roosevelt and the Struggle Over the Arms Embargo.* Chicago: Quadrangle Press, 1962.

Diggins, John P. *Mussolini and Fascism, The View from America.* Princeton: Princeton University Press, 1972.

Dineen, Joseph F. *The Purple Shamrock: The Honorable James Michael Curley of Boston.* New York: W.W. Norton, 1949.

Enloe, Cynthia. *Ethnic Conflict and Political Development.* Boston: Little, Brown & Co., 1973.

Fanon, Frantz. *The Wretched of the Earth.* Translated by Constance Farrington. New York: Grove Press, 1968.

Fuchs, Lawrence. *Political Behavior of American Jews.* Glencoe, Ill.: The Free Press, 1956.

Gambino, Richard. *Blood of My Blood, The Dilemma of Italian Americans.* Garden City, N.Y.: Doubleday, 1975.

Gans, Herbert J. *The Urban Villagers, Group and Class in the Life of Italian Americans.* New York: The Free Press, 1962.

Geertz, Clifford. *The Interpretation of Cultures.* New York: Basic Books, 1973.

Glazer, Nathan, and Moynihan, Daniel P. *Beyond the Melting Pot.* 2d ed. Cambridge: the M.I.T. Press, 1970.

Gordon, Milton M. *Assimilation in American Life.* New York: Oxford University Press, 1964.

Grant, Ronald, and Wellhofer, S., eds. *Ethnonationalism, Multinational Corporations and the Modern State.* Denver: University of Denver Monograph Series on World Affairs, 1979.

Greeley, Andrew M. *The American Catholic, A Social Portrait.* New York: Basic Books, 1977.

_____. *Ethnicity in the United States: A Preliminary Reconnaissance.* New York: John Wiley & Sons, 1974.

_____. *That Most Distressful Nation, The Taming of American Irish.* Chicago: Quadrangle Books, 1972.

Handlin, Oscar. *Boston's Immigrants, A Study in Acculturation.* Rev.
    and enl. ed., New York: Atheneum, 1970.
_____. *Race and Nationality.* Garden City, N.Y.: Doubleday, 1957.
Hechter, Michael. *Internal Colonialism, The Celtic Fringe and British
    National Development, 1536-1966.* Los Angeles: University of
    California Press, 1975.
Herberg, Will. *Protestant-Catholic-Jew, An Essay in American Religious
    Sociology.* Garden City, N.Y.: Doubleday, 1955.
Higham, John. *Strangers in the Land, Patterns of American Nativism
    1860-1925.* New York: Atheneum, 1974.
Hofstadter, Richard. *The Age of Reform.* New York: Random House,
    1955; Vintage Press, 1970.
Huthmacher, J. Joseph. *Massachusetts People and Politics 1919-1933.*
    Cambridge: Harvard University Press, 1959.
Isaacs, Harold. *Idols of the Tribe, Group Identity and Political Change.*
    New York: Harper & Row, 1975.
Jackson, Kenneth T. *The Ku Klux Klan in the City, 1915-1930.* New York:
    Oxford University Press, 1967.
Kammen, Michael. *People of Paradox.* New York: Random House; Vintage
    Press, 1972.
Kennedy, Rose Fitzgerald. *Times to Remember.* Garden City, N.Y.:
    Doubleday, 1974.
Keohane, Robert O., and Nye, Joseph S., Jr. *Power and Interdependence.*
    Boston: Little, Brown & Co., 1976.
_____. *Transnational Relations and World Politics.* Cambridge: Harvard
    University Press, 1971.
Kramer, Judith R. *The American Minority Community.* New York:
    Thomas Y. Crowell Co., 1970.
Levin, Murray B. *The Alienated Voter, Politics in Boston.* New York:
    Holt, Rinehart & Winston, 1960.
Lubbell, Samuel. *The Future of American Politics.* 3d ed. New York:
    Harper & Row, 1963.
Lupo, Alan. *Liberty's Chosen Home, The Politics of Violence in Boston.*
    Boston: Little, Brown & Co., 1977.
Mann, Arthur. *Yankee Reformers in the Urban Age.* Cambridge: Harvard
    University Press, 1954.
Marcus, Sheldon. *Father Coughlin, The Tumultous Life of the Priest of the
    Little Flower.* Boston: Little, Brown & Co., 1973.
McCaffrey, Lawrence J. *The Irish Diaspora in America.* Bloomington:
    Indiana University Press, 1976.
Merwick, Donna. *Boston Priests 1848-1910, A Study in Social and Intel-
    lectual Change.* Cambridge: Harvard University Press, 1973.

Newman, William M. *American Pluralism, A Study of Minority Groups and Social Theory*. New York: Harper & Row, 1973.

Novak, Michael. *The Rise of the Unmeltable Ethnics, The New Political Force of the Seventies*. New York: Macmillan Co., 1971.

O'Brien, David J. *American Catholics and Social Reform, The New Deal Years*. New York: Oxford University Press, 1968.

O'Connor, Thomas H. *Bibles, Brahmins, and Bosses, A Short History of Boston*. Boston: Trustees of the Boston Public Library of the City of Boston, 1976.

O'Donnell, Kenneth P.; Powers, David F.; and McCarthy, Joe. *Johnny, We Hardly Knew Ye, Memories of John Fitzgerald Kennedy*. Boston: Little, Brown & Co., 1970.

Park, Robert E. *Race and Culture*. New York: The Free Press, 1945.

Rose, Richard. *Governing Without Consensus, An Irish Perspective*. Boston: Beacon Press, 1971.

Said, Abdul Aziz, ed. *Ethnicity and U.S. Foreign Policy*. New York: Praeger, 1977.

Said, Abdul A., and Simmons, Luis R., eds. *Ethnicity in an International Context*. New Brunswick, N.J.: Transaction Books, 1976.

Schermerhorn, R.A. *Comparative Ethnic Relations, A Framework for Theory and Research*. New York: Random House, 1970.

Shibutani, Tamotsu, and Kian Kawn. *Ethnic Stratification, A Comparative Approach*. New York: Macmillan Co., 1965.

Soloman, Barbara M. *Ancestors and Immigrants, A Changing New England Tradition*. Cambridge: Harvard University Press, 1956.

Stack, John F., Jr., ed. *Ethnic Identities in a Transnational World: Preliminary Assessments*. Westport, Conn.: Greenwood Press, forthcoming.

Sterling, Richard W. *Macropolitics, International Relations in a Global Society*. New York: Alfred A. Knopf, 1974.

Suhrke, Astri, and Noble, Lela., eds. *Ethnic Conflict in International Relations*. New York: Praeger, 1978.

Suttles, Gerald D. *The Social Order of the Slum, Ethnicity and Territory in the Inner City*. Chicago: University of Chicago Press, 1970.

Thernstrom, Stephen. *The Other Bostonians, Poverty and Progress in the American Metropolis 1880-1970*. Cambridge: Harvard University Press, 1973.

Thorson, Thomas Landon. *Biopolitics*. New York: Holt, Rinehart & Winston, 1970.

Tull, Charles J. *Father Coughlin and the New Deal*. Syracuse, N.Y.: Syracuse University Press, 1965.

van den Berghe, Pierre L. *Race and Racism, A Comparative Perspective*.

New York: John Wiley & Sons, 1967.

Waltz, Kenneth N. *Man, the State and War, A Theoretical Analysis.* New York: Columbia University Press, 1958.

Warner, Sam Bass, Jr. *Streetcar Suburbs, The Process of Growth in Boston 1870-1900.* Cambridge: Harvard University Press and M.I.T. Press, 1962.

Whyte, William F. *Street Corner Society, The Social Structure of an Italian Slum.* Chicago: Chicago University Press, 1943.

Wirth, Louis. *The Ghetto.* Chicago: University of Chicago Press, 1928.

Woods, Robert A., ed. *Americans in Process, A Settlement Study.* Boston: Houghton, Mifflin & Co., 1902.

Woods, Robert A., and Kennedy, Albert J. *The Zone of Emergence.* Cambridge: M.I.T. Press, 1962.

ARTICLES

Barth, Fredrik. Introduction to *Ethnic Groups and Boundaries,* edited by Fredrik Barth, pp. 9-38. Boston: Little, Brown & Co., 1969.

Bayor, Ronald H. "Italians, Jews and Ethnic Conflict." *International Migration Review* 6 (Winter 1972): 372-84.

Bell, Daniel. "Ethnicity and Social Change." In *Ethnicity, Theory and Experience,* edited by Nathan Glazer and Daniel P. Moynihan, pp. 141-70. Cambridge: Harvard University Press, 1975.

Birenbaum, Arnold, and Greer, Edward. "Toward a Structural Theory of the Contemporary Working Class Culture." *Ethnicity* 3 (March 1976): 4-18.

Bushee, Frederick A. "The Invading Host." In *Americans in Process,* edited by Robert A. Woods, pp. 40-69. Boston: Houghton, Mifflin & Co., 1902.

Connor, Walker. "Nation-Building or Nation-Destroying." *World Politics* 24, no. 1 (April 1972): 319-55.

_____. "The Politics of Ethnonationalism." *Journal of International Affairs* 27, no. 1 (1973): 1-19.

Dashefsky, Arnold. "Theoretical Frameworks in the Study of Ethnic Identity: Toward a Social Psychology of Ethnicity." *Ethnicity* 2 (March 1975): 10-19.

Du Bois, W.E.B. "The Inter-Racial Implications of the Ethiopian Crisis, A Negro View." *Foreign Affairs* 14 (October 1935): 74-87.

Edmondson, Locksley. "Caribbean Nation-Building and the Internationalization of Race: Issues and Perspectives." In *Ethnicity and Nation-Building: Comparative, International and Historical Perspectives,* edited by Wendell Bell and Walter E. Freeman, pp. 73-84. Beverly Hills: Sage Publications, 1974.

Enloe, Cynthia H. "Multinational Corporations in the Making and Unmaking of Ethnic Groups." In *Ethnonationalism, Multinational Corporations and the Modern World,* edited by Ronald Grant and S. Wellhofer. Denver: University of Denver Monograph Series on World Affairs, 1979.

Francis, E.K. "The Nature of the Ethnic Group." *American Journal of Sociology* 52 (March 1947): 391-408.

Glazer, Nathan. "The Universalization of Ethnicity." In *At Issue, Politics in the World Arena,* edited by Steven L. Spiegel, pp. 53-65. New York: St. Martin's Press, 1977.

Greenstone, J. David. "Ethnicity, Class, and Discontent, The Case of Polish Peasant Immigrants." *Ethnicity* 2 (March 1975): 1-9.

Higham, John. "Integration vs. Pluralism, Another American Dilemma." *The Center Magazine* 6 (July-August 1974): 63-70.

Huntington, Samuel P. "Transnational Organizations in World Politics." *World Politics* 25, no. 3 (April 1973): 333-67.

Isajiw, Wsevold W. "Definitions of Ethnicity." *Ethnicity* 1 (July 1974): 111-24.

Kaiser, Karl. "Transnational Politics: Toward a Theory of Multinational Politics." *International Organization* 25, no. 4 (Autumn 1971): 790-817.

Keohane, Robert O., and Nye, Joseph S., Jr. "Transnational Relations and World Politics: A Conclusion." In *Transnational Relations and World Politics,* edited by Robert O. Keohane and Joseph S. Nye, Jr., pp. 375-89. Cambridge: Harvard University Press, 1971.

Kilson, Martin. "Blacks and Neo-Ethnicity in American Political Life." In *Ethnicity, Theory and Experience,* edited by Nathan Glazer and Daniel P. Moynihan, pp. 236-66. Cambridge: Harvard University Press, 1975.

Le Melle, Tilden J., and Shepherd, George W., Jr. "Race in the Future of International Relations." *Journal of International Affairs* 15 (1971): 302-13.

Nye, Joseph S., Jr., and Keohane, Robert O. "Transnational Relations and World Politics: An Introduction." In *Transnational Relations and World Politics,* edited by Robert O. Keohane and Joseph S. Nye, Jr., pp. ix-xxv. Cambridge: Harvard University Press, 1971.

Patterson, Orlando. "Context and Choice in Ethnic Allegiance: A Theoretical Framework and Caribbean Case Study." In *Ethnicity, Theory and Experience,* edited by Nathan Glazer and Daniel P. Moynihan, pp. 305-49. Cambridge: Harvard University Press, 1975.

Petersen, William. "On the Subnations of Western Europe." In *Ethnicity,*

Theory and Experience, edited by Nathan Glazer and Daniel P. Moynihan, pp. 177-208. Cambridge: Harvard University Press, 1975.

Plax, Martin. "On Group Behavior and the Ethnic Factor in Politics." *Ethnicity* 1 (October 1974): 295-316.

Rosenau, James N. "Introduction: Political Science in a Shrinking World." In *Linkage Politics, Essays on the Convergence of National and International Systems,* edited by James N. Rosenau, pp. 3-14. New York: The Free Press, 1969.

———. "Toward the Study of National-International Linkages." In *Linkage Politics, Essays on the Convergence of National and International Systems,* edited by James N. Rosenau, pp. 38-57. New York: The Free Press, 1969.

Sondermann, Fred A. "The Linkage Between Foreign Policy and International Politics." In *International Politics and Foreign Policy, A Reader in Research and Theory,* edited by James N. Rosenau, pp. 9-29. New York: The Free Press of Glencoe, 1961.

Stack, John F., Jr. "Ethnicity, Racism, and Busing in Boston: The Boston Irish and School Desegregation." *Ethnicity* 6 (March 1979): 21-28.

Stegner, Wallace. "The Radio Priest and His Flock." In *The Aspirin Age 1919-1941,* edited by Isabel Leighton, pp. 246-69. New York: Simon & Schuster, 1949.

Walsh, David I. "Keep America Out of War." *Vital Speeches* 5 (May 15, 1939): 451-52.

Weber, Max. "Ethnic Groups." In *Theories of Society,* edited by Talcott Parsons et al., and translated by Ferdinand Kolegar, pp. 304-11. Glencoe: The Free Press, 1965.

Whyte, William F. "Race Conflicts in the North End of Boston." *New England Quarterly* 12 (December 1939): 623-42.

Woods, Robert A. "Assimilation: A Two Edge Sword." In *Americans in Process, A Settlement Study,* edited by Robert A. Woods, pp. 356-83. Boston: Houghton, Mifflin & Co., 1902.

———. "Metes and Bounds." In *Americans in Process,* edited by Robert A. Woods, pp. 1-10. Boston: Houghton, Mifflin & Co., 1902.

———. "Traffic in Citizenship." In *Americans in Process,* edited by Robert A. Woods, pp. 147-89. Boston: Houghton, Mifflin & Co., 1902.

Index

ABOUT THE AUTHOR

John F. Stack, Jr., is Assistant Professor of Political Science at Florida International University. He is editor of *Ethnic Identities in a Transnational World* (forthcoming, Greenwood Press).